WADSWORTH PHILOSOPHERS SERIES

W9-BZW-393

# ON

# DERRIDA

**Stephen Hahn**
William Paterson University

**WADSWORTH**

TM

**THOMSON LEARNING**

Australia • Canada • Mexico • Singapore • Spain
United Kingdom • United States

# Acknowledgments

I want to thank Dan Kolak for insisting that I write this book, and for continuing to believe it could be done.

I am grateful also to the following friends and colleagues: Eric Steinhart for his close and thoughtful reading of most of the manuscript in its later stages; listeners to a reading of a portion of it at the Philosophy Colloquium at William Paterson University for probing questions—among them Peter Mandik, John Peterman, Richard Rumana, and Stephen Thompson; Kara Rabbitt for supportive comments and confirmation of some details; David Shapiro for the stimulus of conversation and news of his own Derridean exploits; John Koontz for continuing friendship and for pointing me toward further references; and Carmen Pardo for assisting again with formatting the text.

Chrystena and Margaret Mei have provided space apart from daily life in which to complete this work and a space celled "home" to share.

This is dedicated to our daughter Margaret [Ji] Mei, born in the city of Ji An, Jiang Xi Province, and to a generation of Chinese daughters in America: "God chose what is foolish in the world to shame the wise; God chose what is weak in the world to shame the strong." May we know in each other what is foolish and wise, weak and strong, and grow in love.

Waldwick, New Jersey
January 2001

## A Note on the Text

References generally follow the Modern Language Association author and short title format. Dates of first publication of works have been included where they are relevant. Diacritical marks, such as accent marks in French, have been silently deleted, and the very little Greek has been transliterated.

# Contents

# Preface

Jacques Derrida is a complex figure in the course of philosophical discourse from the 20th into the 21st century. This book attempts not to be reductive but to provide a succinct exposition of some principal "places of concentration" in Derrida's writing for readers with an interest in what is often called "post-modern" thought.

The first two chapters provide different kinds of introductions to Derrida, one conceptual or analytical and one narrative. Chapter One focuses on a particular moment in Derrida's public career and provides an analytical summary of his address "Structure, Sign, and Play in the Discourse of the Human Sciences"(1966). One could consider it a snapshot of a Derrida's position at that time—outlines of which could be projected onto other Derridean moments to trace the play of his thought. Chapter Two is more like a narrative that looks at Derrida in the context of his own history and cultural context; not to identify Derrida with particular points of origin, but again to outline the play of identifications from moment to moment in a number of his autobiographical writings. Depending on your predilections as a reader, one or the other of these chapters may better serve you as an introduction to Derrida.

The next two chapters concern Derrida first in relation to two important Continental European philosophers, Edmund Husserl and Martin Heidegger, and then in relation to some aspects of Anglo-American philosophy. Chapter Three reads Derrida's relation to "Western metaphysics" as it is reprised and interrogated in the writings of Husserl and Heidegger and in his encounters with them—and counters all too common popular reports that he wants to put an end to philosophy "once and for all" (Strathern 61). Chapter Four discusses Derrida's Anglo-American relations from the perspective of the resistance in modern philosophy in England and America to over-arching schemes and theories which may again be identified with "metaphysics"—a resistance evident in movements called "logical positivism" and "ordinary language" philosophy, and in some varieties of pragmatism.

In a brief concluding chapter, I suggest that NEITHER the vaunted values of synthesis or compromise NOR those of the either/or (throughout, a principal logical premise of classical Western metaphysics) are ones we should appeal to in appraising Derrida's encounter with philosophy.

Finally, there is a Glossary at the back of the book that a reader can refer to for brief entries on a handful of words that stand out as particularly significant in and around Derrida's writing: In reading these "definitions," the reader will find a kind of circulation of meaning from one term to another, as various terms appear to be near heteronyms for yet others, reflecting Derrida's avoidance of a single analytic vocabulary and resistance to the reification of the paths of his own thinking—or traces of his own memory and writing.

It is frequently the case in Derrida's writing that passages will suggest not only the topic immediately at hand and the most immediate or common referents of the words deployed, but other and more distantly imaged or voiced meanings. For instance, when topics like "substitution" or "the surrogate" arise, one often hears undertones of the story of Abraham and Isaac or a motif of Christian theology. (See Eugene Vance's remarks on the resonance of Augustinian theology in Derrida's writing and Derrida's reply in "Roundtable on Autobiography," in *The Ear of the Other* 80-84; or, Bruce Ellis Benson's review, "Traces of God: The Faith of Jacques Derrida," *Books and Culture* [September/October 2000] 42-45). Tempting as it would be to re-narrate Derrida within a given conceptual framework I have resisted more univocal definition of such themes and tendencies in order to highlight Derrida's resistance to canonical interpretation (to conformity to a pre-determined set of beliefs) and they way in which this resistance, coupled with allusiveness, enlivens his readings and interrogations of Western philosophy and, later more frequently, sacred texts.

The conversations Derrida encourages and engages in almost always end in a sort of irresolution and promise to re-open. To some readers this is frustrating. Clearly it is challenging, all the more so because frequently there are resolutions one has already come to by inheritance that are being challenged without one quite knowing what is being challenged and questioned. It is easier to characterize, and still easier to caricature, Derrida than it is actually to read him, and it is important to keep in mind that de-stabilizing certainty has as important a role in philosophy as the creation of certainty.

Different readers have come to different judgments regarding the relevance of Derrida's strategies and concerns. I hope these pages assist you as a reader by articulating some of those concerns for such evaluation.

# Chapter 1
## Derrida: First Encounter

"I don't believe that there is any perception."—Jacques Derrida, "Structure, Sign and Play: Discussion," *The Structuralist Controversy* (272)

### A Gambit

In the Fall of 1966, Jacques Derrida was among a group of European scholars—philosophers, literary critics, anthropologists, psychoanalysts, and others—who formed the nucleus of discussants at a conference at The Johns Hopkins University. The title of the symposium was "The Languages of Criticism and the Sciences of Man," though the title was given, as the papers predominantly were, in French (Macksey and Donato, "Preface to the First Edition," *The Structuralist Controversy* xv-xix). The topic addressed was "structure" and the "structuralism" or "structuralist" methodology that was prominently recognized in the ethnography of Claude Levi-Strauss and, earlier, in the linguistics of Ferdinand de Saussure. This structuralism had superseded post-war existentialism and phenomenology as a dominant trend in European philosophy, centered in France, as methodology in the "human sciences" to organize the data of empirical inquiry. But it had also become for these scholars a background from which they were quickly distancing themselves. Those who would later be known as "post-structuralists," Derrida being one of the most famous (along with the psychoanalyst Jacques Lacan and semiotician Roland Barthes), were appearing as if under a double sign of structuralism/post-structuralism, and this critical juncture was implied when the proceedings were eventually published in English as *The*

1

Derrida: First Encounter

*Structuralist Controversy.*
Derrida was little-known in the United States at the time and his address—"Structure, Sign, and Play in the Discourse of the Human Sciences" (*Structuralist Controversy* 247-272)—is a model of economy and directness (in contrast to other more oblique writings later). It seems in retrospect to have as its aim the exposition of a position relative to the concept of "structure"—as direct an exposition of a Derridean "position" as one might find—granting that any philosopher evolves, complicates, and redefines positions over time. At the conclusion of his talk, he engaged in give-and-take with a number of discussants that concluded with a remarkable statement:

> Perception is precisely a concept, a concept of an intuition or of a given originating from the thing itself, present itself in its meaning, independently from language, from the system of reference. And I believe that perception is interdependent with the concept of origin and of center and consequently whatever strikes at the metaphysics of which I have spoken strikes also at the very heart of perception. I don't believe that there is any perception. ("Structure, Sign, and Play" 272)

Such a statement is probably disconcerting to most general readers, and even to most readers schooled in Western philosophy as well. Perception is something that we generally do believe in, philosophers or not. And the history of Western philosophy includes a number of positions that involve perception as a keystone not only to epistemology (foundational to modern and early modern philosophy) but to metaphysics as well. For Western metaphysics often hinges on a view that "to be is to be perceived" (Berkeleyan idealism) or that to perceive is to have being (Cartesian rationalism, arguably, which assures us that "cogito, ergo sum" where the "cogito" because it perceives something, if only its own fabulations, is said "to be"). Moreover, it is a common enough feeling for all of us that our "being" is in some sense determined or at least conditioned by our *being recognized—that is, perceived—by an other.* Such a position would be as contemporary, at least, as the European existentialism dominant in the period of Derrida's early engagement with philosophy and modified in the psychoanalysis of Jacques Lacan (see Lacan's essay "Of Structure as an Inmixing..." in *Structuralist Controversy* 186-200).

A typical response to some of the questions that philosophy raises for us in our initial encounters (especially, say, with a Berkeley or a Descartes or a Sartre) is to be disconcerted and even to experience a

2

Derrida: First Encounter
kind of intellectual vertigo. How much more so here. If you take away
perception, don't you take away myself—how do I know myself, find
myself in the world and my way around in the world, my certainty and
my ability to speak? Or where shall I return to and get my bearings?
Isn't it a paradox for someone to speak confidently of there not being
any perception? How could one "know" this without perception? Or is
this a word-game that will turn out to say something different? Is it a
gambit, as in the opening move of a game, that will put us off-guard
and off-center but which will lead us through the usual paces back to
where the usual story—of science, of self-knowledge, of the truth-value
of propositions, and of all that—will be reinstated in a slightly more
refined way, but reinstated nonetheless?

To say either "yes" or "no" would be to foreclose on what is put
in play ("en jeu")—a favorite metaphor of Derrida, reportedly once an
avid soccer player—before we have even seen what the implications of
the statement are or what is at stake in this position. It would also be,
perhaps, to emphasize too much the singularity of Derrida himself, who
is about the business of trying to convince his readers that he is talking
about something in which they are already involved, whether they
know it or not.

**An Opening Act**

Let us consider the Johns Hopkins address an opening act in
Derrida's Anglo-American career, and one that performs an exposition
of much of what will be at stake in succeeding acts of his career. [But
let us also note that the dramatic metaphor may promise more closure
than will follow.]

To explicate its background: The concept of "structure" was
adopted explicitly in the "discourse of the human sciences" as a
methodological concept to compare phenomena of variable content
with respect to a formal category that is not immediately self-evident in
their content. For instance, different existing languages might be
structurally analogous in some way to allow us to study them
(analytically or with an aim to learning to speak or read them) more
efficiently, as in Saussure's linguistics. So, also, the myths of various
cultures might have similar sorts of invariant structures or structural
features, as in the developments in cultural anthropology following
Levi-Strauss. And there might be structural analogies between levels of
operation or intention in a field of phenomena, as for instance between
the structural patterns for generating sentences (syntax) and the
structural rules for telling stories according to or in certain genres
(narrative), as in various schemes of semiotic analysis. One could, as

3

well, compare different sorts of organization, on the basis of "structure"—social exchange, economies, buildings, natural objects, etc. Even philosophies. Such schemata were explored with some intensity throughout the later twentieth century in philosophy, the social sciences, and literary studies.

So deployed, the concept appears to relieve the thinker of asserting one particular language, or one mythology or culture, as the dominant or paradigmatic case against which all others must be defined and evaluated.

But immediately on application of the concept of structure to any phenomena or entities one encounters some problematic questions: Is structure a metaphor or perspective-making device that is used for certain purposes, like a tool, and retired when not in use? Do structures inhere in phenomena or in the mentality of the speaker, "perceiver," thinker? If so, are the structures separate, as idealities or timeless essences would be, from the things structured? Do they exist as formal causes, necessary conditions, accidental similarities, etc.? Are structural similarities between languages referable to the "hard-wiring" of organisms speaking languages? Is the language of structure a meta-language of ideas, of cognition, or of reality? Almost at once, we are involved in metaphysical questions. We are, one could say, involved in a kind of regressive attempt to restructure what is given within the schema of what is said and thought and therefore to repeat the historical effort of Western philosophy.

Derrida's approach to the concept of structure in "Structure, Sign, and Play" is to consider it initially at the highest level of generality, to consider the "structurality of structure"(247). That is, given a concept of "structure," he raises the question of what identifies it as "structure" and not something else, and what is invariant to the concept as it is deployed. It is, he says, that "although it has always been involved [in the play of phenomena—SH], [it] has always been reduced, and this by a process of giving it a center or referring it to a point of presence, a fixed origin"(247). "Structure" may imply an organization in which subordinate elements are variable with respect to some other fixed element. A circle, for instance, though this is not an example he cites in just this way, may be composed of "points" equidistant from its "center," but the requirement of equal distance and of a center are invariable; or a nuclear family (again he does not give this sort of explanatory or pedagogical example) may include any number of children and a present or absent father and mother, but it must conceptually hold these elements about a center (the difference/sameness between parental and filial bond, and the absent

4

center of incest prohibition) or it is not the structure we would call a nuclear family. "The organizing principle of the structure" does not rigidly fix (else it would not have the range of applicability we associate with the concept), but it does "limit what we might call the *freeplay* of the structure" ("Structure, Sign, and Play" 247-48). In a move that will become recognizable in many of Derrida's texts—a kind of signature having the same quality that he analyzes in the concept of "the signature"—a structure both opens up and forecloses this "freeplay." A "structure lacking any center represents the unthinkable itself," while

> the center also closes off the freeplay it opens up and makes possible. *Qua* center, it is the point at which the substitution of contents, elements, or terms is no longer possible. ("Structure" 248)

A structure, as distinct from a mere aggregate or collection of data, requires a center at the same time that such a center is not subject to structurality itself, but is both outside and inside the structure (organizes and so far conceptually supersedes and controls it while remaining connected to and in tension with it)—"origin" or "end," "*arche*" or "*telos*"(248)—determining the indeterminate. The concept is only coherent within this contradiction, expressed in a variety of ways, which posits the "center" as something that definition to variable elements while itself remaining essentially "out of play."

One has to assume that the reader or listener is meant to supply what we would normally call "analogous" instances or examples of the concept actually in play. For instance, the Aristotelian notion (however simplified for purposes of exposition) that organized movement requires a first movement to dis-equilibrate what was not moving and not organized around this first movement. Or, the first Word, which was not just word but primal, authorizing, center of proliferating words. "Successively," Derrida says, "the center receives different forms or names," but "its matrix....is the determination of being as *presence* in all senses of this word"(249). In other words, multiple iterations of the concept of structure, deployed without the concept of structure having been thought through, arise to master an "anxiety" that "is invariably the result of a certain mode of being implicated in the game, of being caught by the game"(248). Another word for the mastery of this anxiety/desire would be "certainty," which (it is not stated but implied here) is a name for the object of classical philosophical inquiry. To be certain, either as subject or object, would be to stand outside what is

5

variable and therefore uncertain. It would be to perceive, at the least,
and perhaps to be able to give an account of, the origin and end of what
is variable.

[We should not assume that Derrida is conducting an analysis of
the everyday use of words such as "certainty" or "perception," and this
is important to note for several reasons. First, such an assumption
would make him speak in the mode of a positive metaphysics where he
does not: He is not about correcting the way you or I commonly speak
about our experience (e.g., "I'm certain I saw the knife on the table a
moment ago") in order to make it conform to or form the basis of
another paradigm or calculus of reality. Second, such an assumption
would lead us to mistake his questioning (not his rejection) of
philosophical inquiry as an attempt to climb out of or through language
to philosophical certainty or "perception" by the analysis of everyday
language: On the contrary, his object is to reveal that philosophical
discourse is much more like or much more tethered to the loose and
aleatory discourse of the everyday than it appears to be (hence his
affinity for the writings of James Joyce and the evident hostility for his
work among some Anglo-American philosophers who base their work
in conceptual analysis).]

So far, Derrida's account proceeds as much like a story ("this
happens and then this happens") as like a logical demonstration or
argument ("there is some x such that...") and it *is* a story (leaving aside
here the demonstration of an intersection between the forms of logical
argument and the forms of narrative). It is important for the sake of not
getting lost in it to highlight the narrativity of the passage. For logic is
one of the things called into question in his account (not to mistake this
to say that Derrida lacks a fine grasp of logic), since logic, too (at least
the Aristotelian logic of the either/or and excluded middle), participates
in the metaphysics he is calling into question. So he continues in that
mode in a passage worth quoting at length:

> The event I called a rupture [in the opening paragraph, which
> begins to tell the story of something that happened to the concept
> of structure—SH]...would presumably have come about when the
> structurality of structure had to begin to be thought, that is to say,
> repeated, and this is why I said this disruption was repetition in all
> senses of the word. From then on it became necessary to think the
> law which governed, as it were, the desire for the center in the
> constitution of structure and the process of signification its
> displacements and its substitutions for this law of the central
> presence—but a central presence which has never been itself,

6

Derrida: First Encounter

which has always already been transported outside itself in its surrogate. *The surrogate does not substitute itself for anything which has somehow pre-existed it* [my italics—SH]. From then on it was probably necessary to begin to think that there was no center, that the center could not be thought in the form of a being-present, that the center had no natural locus, that it was not a fixed locus but a function, a sort of non-locus in which an infinite number of sign substitutions come into play. This moment was that in which language invaded the universal problematic; that in which, in the absence of center or origin, everything became discourse.... ("Structure, Sign, and Play" 249)

If this sounds slightly mytho-poetic or religious, then so it is—which is not to say that Plato or Hegel or many philosophers in between do not sound similarly so. It will depend upon some further reading to decide on the pertinence of the myth or narrative. But here we might point the crux of this story in the italicized sentence where the mood of the verb turns from progressive to indicative: "The surrogate does not substitute itself for anything which has somehow pre-existed it." One could object that this is semantically incoherent for the reason that a "surrogate" by definition, properly, and literally must be a substitute for an original, authentic presence—a thing or relation itself. Unless, that is, one already questioned what it means to be literal or proper. The only burden for a person who would so object would be that of making sure that he or she was not also incoherent in his or her own statements. But what does it mean? And does it mean something such as "I don't believe that there is any perception"? [Yes.]

This statement about the surrogate does not imply in the common meaning of the words that nothing pre-exists (in a physical sense) language or the concept of structure. It means, rather, if one construes "the surrogate" as language or the symbolic mediation of structure, that this language or structure or center or law—system of signs—is not a substitute for some (undetermined) perception that pre-exists it. The concept of "existence" is itself derived from the possibility of predication in language, and so the concept of existence depends upon the invention and intervention of language. Whatever else it is, the "surrogate" is not the translation into another form of something to which we have independent and immediate access; we therefore lack the privilege of verifying the surrogate by comparison to that existence. It is something new (hence the use of the word "rupture"). It is a "surrogate" in the sense that it is taken for but is not the same as some other pre-existing entity. Hence the denial of perception.

7

[The reader will perhaps be impatient. Isn't it the purpose of philosophy to clear something up—at least to try to clear it up—about the world? Here we are with something that we can't clearly identify with anything in the world—even "language" doesn't quite seem to express it—"the surrogate." What's that?]

"Discourse" and "structure" are defined by a discontinuity with what is not-discourse or not-structure, but because they are defined negatively (have you ever *seen* "discourse" or "structure"?) they are not pure. "Structure" is impure with respect to any of its customarily opposite terms, such as "material" or even to "non-structure" because it cannot be thought without some assumption that it exists against a background of otherness, of something not-itself, and contains within its iteration the trace of otherness. If Levi-Strauss's use of the concept of "structure" attempts to enable us to escape a certain kind of ethnocentricity (one, for instance, that would interpret other people's mythologies in terms of the degradation of our own mythology), it also returns us to ethnocentricity because it is precisely the product of an historically derived discourse: "whether he wants to or not...the ethnologist accepts into his discourse the premises of ethnocentrism at the very moment when he is employed in denouncing them" and "this necessity is irreducible; it is not a historical contingency"(252). ("Structure" can barely avoid explicitly introducing the natural scientist, engineer, or technologist as a factographic figure behind its analysis.) No one, in short, has shown that "structure" is any less the product of elaborating on ideas and images that come to hand or mind than any other element of discourse. It is simply a matter that it happens to conform itself well to the aims and ends of explanation within a given cultural and historical moment.

This is not, however, to say that there are no possible qualitative differences in thinking, and hence no responsibility for one's thought:

> [For] if nobody can escape this necessity, and if no one is responsible for giving in to it, however little, this does not mean that all the ways of giving in to it are equally pertinent. The quality and fecundity of a discourse are perhaps measured by the critical rigor with which this relationship to the history of metaphysics and to inherited concepts is thought. (252)

[Is "rigor," then, the key qualitative concept in Derrida's own discourse, like "clarity" in others?] Inevitably, none of us can escape the inheritance of prior predications, which is perhaps the closest Derrida comes to citing a universal truth, and each of us is therefore

8

inevitably responsible for working out our relationship to it. (Chapter 2, below, is primarily about Derrida's own relationship to such an inheritance.)

In a move characteristic for Derrida, he turns to Levi-Strauss's own texts to show how the deployment of a concept that attempts to take us out of the play of history and difference—by demonstrating that actual myths always conform an the abstract model or conceptual scheme—returns us to history and difference. On one hand "in the work of Levi Strauss...the respect for structurality, for the internal originality of structure, compels a neutralization of time and history." On the other, "one can ...describe what is peculiar to the structural organization only by not taking into account, in the very moment of this description, its past conditions: by failing to pose the problem of the passage from one structure to another, by putting history in parenthesis" (263). One result of such an approach is ethnocentrically to project upon another "primitive" culture the qualities of timelessness and passivity (but also fullness of being and presence) that are typical of the self-consciously Western view of non-Western cultures. Another result is the internalization of the loss of such a state to the observer in the "structuralist thematic of broken immediateness" as a "sad, negative, nostalgic, guilty, Rousseauist facet of the thinking of freeplay of which Nietzschean affirmation...would be the other side"(264)—and, implicitly, the Derridean side.

The conclusion to this address brings us to a point where we can note how Derrida both participates in and diverges from the philosophical tradition he invokes. Here we can make some tentative generalizations in order to return to them later as points of reference. First Derrida poses what we might call a dilemma:

> There are thus two interpretations of interpretation, of structure, of sign, of freeplay. The one seeks to decipher, dreams of deciphering, a truth or origin which is free from freeplay and from the order of the sign, and lives like an exile the necessity of interpretation. The other, which is no longer turned toward origin, affirms freeplay and tries to pass beyond man and humanism, the name man being the name of that being who, throughout the history of metaphysics to onto-theology—in other words, throughout the history of all his history—has dreamed of full presence, the reassuring foundation, the origin and end of the game. (264-65)

Customarily, a traditional philosopher would seek to resolve or relieve this opposition, to reduce one polar term to the other which, by

9

reference perhaps to some third term or situation or position or context, controls and moderates it so that there is unity. Classically, philosophy attempts to reduce contradiction or multiplicity to unity. In the Hegelian dialectic, for instance (to give an extremely simplified sketch), human knowledge progresses through limited but productive perspectives toward some further point of clarification beyond (a movement called "Aufhebung" in German and "releve" in French).[1] Rather than to choose either alternative, or yet a third that goes beyond and negates or dissolves them, Derrida suggests another position:

> For my part, although these two interpretations must acknowledge and accentuate their difference and define their irreducibility, I do not believe that today there is any question of *choosing*—in the first place because we are here in a region (let's say, provisionally, a region of historicity) where the category of choice seems particularly trivial; and in the second, because we must first try to conceive of the common ground, and the *différance* of this irreducible difference. (265)

The "question" of this "common ground" and "differance" is not yet formulated and in fact cannot be thought within the customary categories and boundaries of the past history of Western philosophy, "a sort of question, call it historical," which can only be conceived (and Derrida points up a series of metaphors of childbirth) "under the species of non-species, in the formless, mute in fact, and terrifying form of monstrosity"(265). He will eventually identify this abiding within apparent contradictions as "aporia," and will invoke an inheritance that sets out the necessity of decision at the same moment that it takes away the possibility of choice at the moment of decision being bound by a logical (programmable) necessity. Decision is taken in the face of and embodies contradiction.

**[An Aside]**
[Some paragraphs and sentences above appear in brackets to indicate that they function like theatrical asides in which a character comments on the action of a play. This is a more formally marked aside to comment on the previous discussion. The reader will perhaps at this point wish himself or herself for the relief of a more definitive statement of *meaning* in the traditional sense—which is exactly what

---

[1] See the Translator's Note on these terms in the version of the address "Differance" in Jacques Derrida, *Margins of Philosophy* 19, n23.

Derrida takes pains to ward off. Thus, an attempt to summarize even so brief an address or essay as "Structure, Sign, and Play" can be a frustrating or an invigorating experience depending on one's tolerance for certain features of Derrida's writing. Two of these features are immediately specifiable:

**Linguistic:** While a characteristic desire in Western philosophy is to pare back the accretions of sense in the deployment of words—to reduce the degree of metaphoricity or ambiguity of discourse—it is characteristic of Derrida's discursive practice to assimilate multiple meanings in the lexical field of his writing without reducing them to precisely the same meaning. For instance, when Derrida writes, famously, of "differance" it is always with an eye to the Freudian "Nachtraglichkeit" (*Beyond the Pleasure Principle*, Chapter V) because of functional or structural similarities, without necessarily endorsing Freud's meaning with reference to literal neuro-psychological or biological processes. Rather than resisting all "sedimentation" of meaning, Derrida strategically and selectively plays off against such sedimentation. While an ideal of Western metaphysics is to find language that is transparent so that the reader will see through the language to a concept or idea or thing that is unproblematic ("a truth or origin which is free from freeplay and the order of the sign"), Derrida resists allowing any of his language to settle toward the appearance of such transparency. Frequently, this resistance is marked in his text either by Derrida or, for Anglo-American readers, his translators, but it is not always so. The linguistic surface of his writing is always complex—one who had not read Husserl or Derrida on Husserl, for instance, would not readily realize that the word "sedimentation" imports a heritage of transcendental phenomenology into Derrida's text. What is more, his play with language sometimes gives the appearance of doing the exact opposite of what it does do. To some readers it could appear that he repeats the habit of the nineteenth-century philology of trying to find the "root" meaning of words by tracing them back to origins, whereas Derrida is instead trying to point up the historicity of discourse, language, and ideas—to show precisely that they are not timeless but historical inventions, much as they may implicate us in apparently timeless (because structurally determined) moments of invention, much as they may appear to invoke transcendent ideas or "idealities."[2]

---

[2] Arguably, some American literary critics called "deconstructionists" fall into this philological habit in a way that Derrida does not.

11

**Rhetorical/Logical**: It is characteristic of Western philosophy to treat the rhetorical form of an utterance as a mere shell or overlay to the logical form, and to conform the rhetorical form to assumptions about logical form. For Derrida, who knows logic as well as anyone, the privileging of Western logical axioms (rules of contradiction and identity) is a strategy of control by which "anxiety [of being implicated in the game] can be mastered"(248) by reference to "a point of presence, a fixed origin"(247) or a "full presence which is out of play" (248). What is questioned is not the consistency of formal logic but the presumption of reference to a unitary point of presence or origin in discourse, which is for Derrida (as he attempts to demonstrate in "White Mythology: Metaphor in the Text of Philosophy") the question over which the opposition of rhetorical/logical, metaphoric/literal arises and is arbitrarily decided in favor of logic and the literal in Western metaphysics. For Western philosophy, propositions of the form "either/or" or "both/and" are favored over propositions of the form "neither/nor" or "not here and not yet." (This is nearly the same as to say that it is a metaphysics of presence.) The conclusion to "Structure, Sign, and Play" turns on a reversal of just this rhetorical/logical ordering, for a "monstrosity" is precisely a "neither/nor" that defies received categories of being. (See the use of this trope in *Of Grammatology* 5.) Historically, the "monstrous" at birth or conception is that which is "neither male nor female" or "neither fish nor fowl"— that is, it is something for which there is no referential category, which defies logic, and yet which "presents itself" (L. "monstrum"). The fault of the favoring of the logical forms "either/or" or "both/and" is that one must consider anything that appears under or within the categories of what is already conceived to exist with reference to an already determined set of decisions about presence/absence, being/non-being. Thus, a pre-decision or pre-disposition toward certain grammatical-logical forms (e.g., "either/or") is identified by Derrida with something called "onto-theology," and it would even consider such a phrasing to be redundant, because it has already decided that "God" ("theo-") is "Being" ("onto-")—a decision that Derrida, atheist or not, would rightly challenge as a presumptive conceptual limitation that does not even accommodate all of what the Western tradition has had to say, speculatively, on the subject of God.[3]]

---

[3] Recent analyses of Derrida's rhetorical and linguistic dispositions include Marian Hobson, *Jacques Derrida: Opening Lines*, and Geoffrey Bennington, "An Idea of Syntax" in *Interrupting Derrida* 180-196).

**Open Ending I**

Derrida ends "Structure, Sign, and Play" not with an assertion of unity-in-difference that stitches together or sutures disparate ideas and phenomena with reference to a "point of presence," not with conceptual closure, but with a gesture toward whatever it is that resists closure and categorization. He ends, that is, with a challenge to "perception." Here as elsewhere he refuses the closure we identify with perception as an act that stands apart from the receding horizons of past and future and what is not present in a moment of pure presence. It is as though in saying "I don't believe that there is any perception," he says that there isn't any (pure) present or any (pure) presence. Indeed, that *is* what he is says. [But what can that mean?] Not because in a metaphysical way there is a kind of Bergsonian flow between some entities defined by these terms, but because discourse or language (the signifying system) is what enables us to mark time and the marking of time is (1) always delayed, never on-center with a non-linguistic experience (consider the temporal experience of the autistic, what is it?), and (2) always marked in discourse by verbal shifters which are constantly open to re-contextualizing. Language itself, which articulates the difference of moments, the "surrogate" for something that perhaps does not exist (the phenomena it points to), always differs with respect to the moment it names. It does not arrive at a conclusion (a non-linguistic point of presence or perception). What Western philosophy attempts to do is by language to arrive at a conclusion. But the conclusion does not arrive. Life goes on. Yet life does not go on without the prospect of arrival.

# Chapter 2
## Derrida's Resume

"what is peacefully called a language...."—Jacques Derrida, *Monolingualism of the Other* (17)

**Backstory**

Classical Hollywood films often use a technique called romantic narration in which a subjective "voiceover" leads us into a scopically "objective" scene of conflict whose origin and genesis is unknown to us and therefore not fully interpretable. Relationships among the characters and the nature of conflicts among them, and within a central hero, are enigmatic until some "piece of the puzzle" from the past is discovered and the nature of the characters and their relationships is revealed. Movies such as "Citizen Kane," "Mildred Pierce," and "Marnie" are particularly good examples of the genre, and the narrative in each is based in a life story. Perhaps, however, this form of narration is as old as Sophocles' "Oedipus." The form of such stories activates and depends upon a thematics of presence. Perhaps also we live our lives, necessarily, thinking that some missing piece will complete it (for good or ill) and bring it to closure—and yet.... A narrative that imposes one "piece" that ties together all the other pieces participates in the "logocentrism" of Western metaphysics—like a structure that depends upon a center that is and is not part of the structure, that transcends and underwrites the authenticity of the structure. From the Lacanian perspective, off-center both to Freud and to Derrida's assimilation of Freud in deconstruction ("differance" and *Nachtraglicheit*), such completion is death, which is desired and yet not desired too much. Among many forms of telling the story of a life, this one which

14

imposes a center and a structure has a great deal of ideological strength in our culture.

Derrida poses some particular problems for the telling of a story about his own life, not the least of which is his resistance to any format that would allow it to be told in one register as the story of one life in which a missing piece can be supplied to make it whole. Indeed, he rightly says of telling his own story:

> In its common concept, autobiographical anamnesis [un-forgetting—SH] pre-supposes *identification*. And precisely not identity. No, an identity is never given, received, or attained; only the interminable and indefinitely phantasmic process of identification endures. (*Monolingualism* 28)

This statement is bound to seem especially odd to American readers for whom the term "identity" is a more commonplace, but not more authentic, term of self-reference than "identification" (with its connotations of temporality and temporary-ness, even irony). Derrida, being *precise* here, points out that in memory or introspection we identify with a differing and deferred image of self, a phantasm that escapes final determination as the one-true-thing about us (cf. Lacan, "Of Structure as an Inmixing...." 194). If I read some of Derrida's later religiously-oriented writings clearly enough, while he denies the possibility of attaining such wholeness of "identity," he also denies the ability to vacate or transcend the desire for such wholeness (the impetus for the process of identification). That is, in one sense, his way of telling the story. You will perhaps notice also that it repeats the "neither/nor" formula or *aporia* discussed in the Chapter 1, since it is possible neither to attain the desire nor to escape the desire. Within an incomplete story, elements must be less decisive than in a completed one. They are parts and figures that have some significance, more or less than chance, but they do not supply their own meaning, and we do not arrive at an identity. Again, "we do not arrive" could be a sort of Derridean motto or mantra. In any essentially open story, in which there is no one totally decisive moment (no absolute center), the meaning and significance of elements of the story change with the addition of new elements, including not only events but perspectives and points of view; but they do not therefore lose all meaning and significance by being open to such revision.

Derrida has written autobiographically in several formats, and often inter-textually in a kind of reverie, as in the running intertext of *Jacques Derrida* by Geoffrey Bennington and Jacques Derrida, or in the Rousseauist essay form of *Monolingualism of the Other; or, The Prosthesis of Origin*, in *The Post-Card* and in *Glas*. (He has, as well, participated in a "Roundtable on Autobiography" with Rodolphe Gasche et al, transcribed in *The Ear of the Other* 39-89.) Such texts provide suggestions and insights that the reader may want to consider alongside more straightforward chronological rendering, such as that provided by Bennington's "Curriculum Vitae" (*Jacques Derrida* 325-336). My approach in supplying this brief biographical backstory to our examination of Derrida's philosophy is to try to provide a broad framework that places Derrida in a historical moment and to explicate a few identifying statements made about him, with an "aside" on the question of how or why biography should matter at all regarding a *philosopher*. In a sense, Derrida's biography illustrates something about deconstruction and textuality, as we will see.

## Vita However Brevis

Derrida is a "French philosopher" (*Cambridge Dictionary of Philosophy*) who was born in El-Biar, Algeria to an assimilated Sephardic Jewish family in 1930. This bare sentence and sentences further on state conditions that are nothing other than textual effects or identifications, which depend on other texts and identifications. Without textuality, without language, there is no "French" or "France," no Sephardim, no Jew, no Algeria, and no Jacques Derrida: "There is not a single signified that escapes, even if recaptured, the play of signifying references that constitute language" (*Of Grammatology* 7); "the name, especially the so-called proper name, is always caught in a chain or system of differences" (*Of Grammatology* 89). None of this, to be as plain as possible, means something like what some of Derrida's detractors sometimes take him to mean. It does not mean that there is no physical or juridical area called France, for "France" is an actual effect of statements that, being articulated, have further effects; but each of these effects is mediated and appears to us through textual mediation which presupposes the signifying system. Otherwise, there is nothing that connects "France" to any determination or effect of meaning. And yet there is also nothing that metaphysically identifies France apart from these textual connections, no ideality (though perhaps people imagine this sentimentally or phantasmically), no center, and no boundary. Likewise, "French." Although Derrida will play with the notion of writing and speaking a purer French than others (*Monolingualism* 46-47), he knows there is no French language as a transcendent object than which to be less pure, no absolute boundary between French and not-French—between literary and demotic forms

16

of a "language" or between one language and another.

[Aside: The dictionary says a "French philosopher," which can be taken to mean simply a philosopher of French nationality or location, but which quickly becomes something else, not irrelevant: A philosopher writing in French (like Descartes in one version of his *Discourse on Method)* or a philosopher in a distinctly French tradition or culture. One model of philosophy, however, would think of the philosopher as attempting think what must be thought by anyone, always and everywhere, without respect to a particular or actual language or nationality—what is universal. There is a necessary tension between this idea of attaining universality and the actuality of history. Aristotle, in one foundational moment for Western philosophy, promulgates the axiom with respect to the multiplicity of languages: "Just as all men have not the same writing so all men have not the same speech sounds, but mental experiences, of which these are the *primary symbols* (*semeia protos*), are also the same for all, as also are those things of which our experiences are the images" [*De Interpretatione* 1, 16a; quoted in *Of Grammatology* 11—JD's italics.]. Considering the philosopher under the figure of "the thinker," Heidegger in *"What is Called Thinking?"* writes:

> A thinker is not beholden to a thinker—rather, when he is thinking, he holds on to what is being thought, to Being. Only insofar as he holds on to Being can he be open to the influx of the thoughts which the thinkers before him have thought. (95; quoted in Gasche 71)

According to this ideal or model, the received text of philosophy—its language—establishes a tradition that is not itself thought. Only independent access to "Being" enables the "influx" of thought, as though thought were already existent apart from language, and language—the received text—were actually a substitute for thought ("not beholden to a thinker"). If I am thinking at all, I am not depending on the language of others.

Thinking, on this view, is radically independent of language or speech and writing in the broadest sense. Thus, the struggle of thinking is to get beyond or perhaps behind language.[4] There is, of course,

---

[4] This is, for instance already a theme in Aristotle's *De Anima* (429a, 12-28), which asserts the non-identical similarity between thinking and perceiving, but insists on a fundamental difference. It reads in part: "Now, if thinking is akin to perceiving, it would either be affected in

17

something intuitively appealing about these two passages. At the same time, however, the history of this tradition is one in which we see philosophers repeatedly returning to distinguish thinking from language without being able to demonstrate thought entirely apart from language. Moreover, as much as we might say themes such as this constitute one over-arching Western philosophical tradition, philosophical traditions do diverge along the lines of demarcation of cultural, national, ethnic, and linguistic differences. To say that Derrida is a "French philosopher" (as complicated as that may be made by the circumstances we are noting in our narrative) is to say that he writes within a tradition that thinks certain themes with certain nuances, differently from a Russian or Anglo-American tradition, say, and in a language (though Derrida is less restricted than some by or defiant of linguistic boundaries) with certain historically determined resources which enable and dispose it to say some things rather than others, and not to say some things as well.]

Derrida's mother's grandfather was born in Algiers in 1832. The family was therefore established in Algeria at the time of the "Crimieux decree in 1870" that granted French citizenship to indigenous Jews. During Derrida's childhood and youth, Algeria remained an Arab country (with reference to population) colonized by France, and the dominant school language was French, the language of political and cultural power. Students studied, as depicted in Albert Camus' short story "The Guest," the culture and geography of France. But during the occupation of France in World War II, Algeria was also an "occupied" country (although German troops never entered it) and subject to anti-Jewish exclusionary laws. These laws and administrative policies and practices result in progressively severe exclusions, from Jews being allowed to attend school but not being allowed to participate in exercises such as ritual flag-raising to their being expelled from school because of quotas more stringent in the colony than in metropolitan France (Bennington 326). Being an assimilated Jew (and referring

---

some way by the object of thought or something else of this kind. It must then be unaffected, but capable of receiving the form, and potentially such as it, although not identical with it; and as that which is capable of perceiving is to the objects of perception, so must be the intellect similarly to its objects. It must, then, since it thinks all things, be unmixed, as Anaxagoras says, in order that it may rule, that is in order that it may know....It must have no other nature than this, that it is potential. That part of the soul, then, called intellect....is actually none of existing things before it thinks."

familiarly to some Judaic rites under a Christian terminology) and only tenuously identified with Judaism religiously, Derrida was denominated a Jew by others, by the law, and by the statement of a classroom teacher that "French culture is not meant for little Jews" (Aouate 126). (He will maintain an "affiliation" with Jewish identity in his adult life, which will mean also a resistance to that identity.) The language of the country, Arabic, was not a "school language" except for a small number of students who expected to become tradespersons; and so, Derrida did not study Arabic, one of the languages of his geographical homeland. (Indeed, he later points to the pathetic tragicomedy of colonialism, exclaiming: "Arabic, an optional foreign language in Algeria!" *Monolingualism* 38.) Being from North Africa but speaking French, and in fact learning a culturally refined form of French through his studies in the Lycee and beyond, Derrida becomes not just "French" in the sense of being a French citizen (which he is) but also "Franco-Maghrebian"—a kind of contradictory political identity/non-identity since "le Maghreb" is a geographical and cutural but not a national designation: There are no citizens of the Maghreb and no precise borders to it. He does and does not belong to anything.

In a long autobiographical meditation in *Monolingualism of the Other*, Derrida speculates on the consequences of the shifts of identification that resulted from the political and administrative edicts of his youth:

I was very young at the time, and I certainly did not understand very well—already, I did not understand very well—what citizenship was and loss of citizenship meant to say. But I do not doubt that exclusion—from the school reserved for young French citizens—could have a relationship to the disorder of identity of which I was speaking to you a moment ago. I do not doubt either that such "exclusions" come to leave their mark upon the belonging or non-belonging *of* language, this affiliation *to* language, this assignation [probably most closely, "legal assignment"—SH] to what is peacefully called a language.

I have just emphasized that the ablation ["taking away"—SH] of citizenship lasted for two years, but it did not, *strictu sensu*, occur "under the Occupation." It was a Franco-French operation, one ought to say even an act of French Algeria in the absence of any German occupation. One never saw a German uniform in Algeria. No alibi, denial, or illusion is possible: it was impossible to transfer the responsibility of that exclusion upon an occupying alien.

We were hostages of the French, enduringly....something of it remains with me, no matter how much I travel. (*Monolingualism* 16-17)

I quote this passage at length to note Derrida's sense of the complexity of his relationship to his first language and nationality, but beyond that to register the sense of agency and responsibility which is sometimes missed in extracting something like doctrines out of Derrida's writing. Granted that the sense of complexity of arrangements determining human freedom, identity, and responsibility is as pronounced as in a fictional representation, Derrida perhaps speaks for many others when he says:

I do not know whether there are other examples of this in the history of modern-nation states, examples of such a deprivation of citizenship decreed for tens and tens of thousands of people at a time. In October 1940, by abolishing the Cremieux decree of October 24, 1870, France herself, the French state in Algeria, the "French state" legally constituted (by the Chamber of the Popular Front!) following the well-known act of parliament, this state was refusing French identity to—rather, taking it away again from—those whose collective memory continued to recollect or had just barely forgotten that it had been lent to them as if only the day before and had not failed to give rise, less than half a century earlier (1898), to murderous persecutions and the beginnings of pogroms. Without, however, preventing an unprecedented "assimilation": profound, rapid, zealous, and spectacular. In two generations. (17)

Perhaps he speaks, that is, both for those on whom similarly violent acts of symbolic deprivation are perpetrated and for those who dwell peacefully within what they assume is a natural identity (as citizenship is frequently considered under categories such as "native," "natural born," and "naturalized" and distinguished, in the United States for instance, from "alien" and "resident alien" identities) which indeed can be both taken and given if circumstances permit:

Along with others, I lost and then gained back French citizenship. I lost it for years without having another. You see, not a single one. I did not ask for anything. I hardly knew at the time, that it

20

had been taken away from me, not, at any rate, in the legal and objective form of knowledge in which I am explaining it here (for, alas, I got to know it in another way [by the experience of being excluded within and then expelled from school—SH]). And then, one day, one "fine day," without, once again, my asking for anything, and still too young to know it in a properly political way, I found the aforementioned citizenship again. The state, to which I never spoke, had given it back to me. The state, which was no longer Petain's "French state," was recognizing me anew. That was, I think, in 1943; I had still never gone "to France"; I had never been there. (16)

Thus, "identity"—French or Jewish or other—is conferred by the acceptance or assignment of others as much or even more so—even absolutely—by the regard and the language of others, and is not "natural." The idea of the loss of "natural" citizenship unmasks the surrogacy of the State, which substitutes for something ("nature") that never previously existed conceptually as such until determined in relation to this substitute ("the State").

It is worth noting and drawing out the implications of Derrida's language (even in translation) here because we might habitually focus on the "objective" or publicly "factual" aspects of this account—the dates and names of laws, for instance—and miss part of what he is telling us about himself, perhaps about ourselves. How many times does he emphasize his youth and lack of knowledge?

"I was very young at the time...."

"I certainly did not understand very well...."

"I lost it for years without having another one."

"I hardly knew at the time...."

"The state, to which I never spoke...."

I take these statements about lack of knowledge, inaction or passivity, and innocence to point up what is by contrast the violence of "what is peacefully called a language"—the law, either formal and explicit, or informal and tacit in the practice of naming. Each is "peaceful" in the sense of being implacable, offering no resources outside itself and not revealing its own history or motivation or admitting anything other than a specifically stated exception.

Many years later, Derrida will express affinities with and support for Nelson Mandela, *Charta 77* in Czechoslovakia (he is a founder of the Jan Hus Association, named after the Czech martyr, and he was jailed in 1981 in Prague on trumped up charges of drug trafficking), and other human rights causes. More immediately, he appears to begin

21

a series of readings in and perhaps identifications with "outsider" philosophers—Rouseau, Gide, Nietzsche, Camus, and Sartre, in his studies at the Lycee de Ben Aknoun (where he had begun study in 1941 and was expelled for reasons of ethnic quotas in 1942) in 1944-47 and then at Lycee Gauthier in 1947-48. By 1949, he is attending the Lycee Louis-le-Grand in Paris and continuing his study of philosophy; but failing entrance examinations for l'Ecole Normale Superieure, he enrolls in *khagne* at Louis-le-Grand (a rigorous post-secondary or *baccalaureat* course of study) with fellow students of some name in later years, notably Pierre Bourdieu and Michel Serres). By 1952, he is attending l'Ecole Normale Superieure and—despite earlier failures and apparent nervous crises—begins progress toward academic success, a "career path," and marriage (he meets his future wife Margaret Aucouturier in 1953, marries her in Boston, Massachusetts, in 1957) He begins work on Husserl in 1953 and visits archives in Switzerland, then writes a Dissertation des Hautes Etudes on "The Problem of Genesis in the Philosophy of Husserl" but fails portions of exams which select candidates for permanent teaching positions in France. After passing the *agregation*, he travels to Harvard University in 1956-57 (where the literary critic Paul de Man is teaching and where numerous post-war U.S. and international scholars in philosophy and literary studies are advanced graduate students).

Complicating the narrative of identification somewhat, Derrida serves mandatory (French) military service in Algeria as a schoolteacher to the children of soldiers—despite his opposition to French colonial rule—in 1957-59, only to see his family evacuated (after his own return to France and a teaching post at Le Mans) in 1962. (He does not return to his boyhood home until 1971, while lecturing at the University of Algiers.) With the publication of his *Edmund Husserl's "Origin of Geometry": An Introduction* (French first edition, 1962), the address at Johns Hopkins (1966), and the publication of *Voice and Phenomena* (in French, 1967) and *De La Grammatologie* (1967), Derrida comes increasingly to the fore in French and international philosophical circles and even, by the 1970s, to attain a kind of celebrity. Yet though he attains both notoriety and recognition, including honorary degrees and honorific teaching positions, he also raises anxieties among many. In 1992, the award of an honorary degree from Cambridge University is marked by a split vote of the faculty on the matter. Despite being appointed to such posts as the Director d'Etudes at l'Ecole Normale Superiere de Sciences Sociales, he is frequently treated as an outsider to the French academic establishment. Like many of his contemporaries, he becomes less identified with his

22

own ambiguous nationality and more cosmopolitan and international.

## But Is He a Philosopher?

Already we have spoken of the model of the philosopher as a thinker for whom language is the almost accidental medium for thought that exists, putatively, outside of language. And partially we have spoken of Derrida's own narrative of himself as implicated in and by language. The response of a philosopher, typically, to the presumed accidents of language is to seek to correct them, to universalize thought behind or carried within or as at any rate distinct from any language in which it is imperfectly revealed or carried. But, as we have by now also partly discovered, Derrida denies that we have access to an "outside" or a "behind" of language, for every attempt to discover what is thought can only lead us to another form of writing or representation or to a space in which nothing is said or thought—"l'abyme," "chasm," or "rupture," being three various terms used to signify the break with and within meaning. Otherwise we are within and implicated in the play of language. As a consequence, perhaps, one of his more sympathetic biographer-critics asserts that "Derrida does not 'do' philosophy, but 'reads' philosophy" (Bennington 285) and invokes the formula of the "neither/nor" to describe his activity (286-87). If his subject is so often philosophy or its adjuncts (law, the philosophy of the literary object, etc.), what is the nature of this "nor"?

Let us return to the autobiographical matrix describing his identifications, located again in another narrative of the genesis of choices and identifications, "out of Algeria," if you will:

> As an adolescent, I no doubt had the feeling that I was living in conditions where it was both difficult and therefore necessary, urgent, to say things that were not allowed, in any case to be interested in those situations in which writers say such things that are not allowed. For me, Algeria in the forties (Vichy, official anti-semitism, the Allied landing at the end of 1942, the terrible colonial repression of Algerian resistance in 1945 at the time of the first serious outbreaks heralding the Algerian war) was not only or primarily my family situation, but it is also true that my interest in literature, diaries, journals in general, signified a typical, stereotypical revolt against the family. My passion for Nietzsche, Rousseau, and also Gide, whom I read a lot at that time, meant among other things: "Families, I hate you." ("This Strange Institution....," *Acts of Literature* 38-39)

This nascent urge, as he depicts it, led to an identification with such writers and to a sort of obviously "Oedipal" revolt that could be considered entirely predictable for an intelligent young man, even in untroubled *petit bourgeois* circumstances:

> I thought of literature as the end of the family, and of the society it represented, even if that family was also, on the other hand, persecuted. Racism was everywhere in Algeria at the time, it was running wild in all directions. Being Jewish and a victim of anti-semitism didn't spare one the anti-Arab racism I felt around me, in manifest or latent form. Literature, or a certain promise of "being able to say everything," was in any case the outline of what was calling me or signaling to me in the situation I was living in at the time, familial and social. (39)

One of the great, if typical, attractions of literature is its betrayal either through plot or figurative language of the expectations laid down by any given social circumstance. It thrives on revealing exactly what the protocols of daily living pass over or explain away, and so it provides a way for an adolescent self to differentiate itself from familial and social expectations. Two of the three writers cited here by Derrida—the novelistic philosopher Rousseau and the philosophical novelistic Gide—represent a particularly pronounced antagonism to assimilation by an established social or symbolic order in forms that also transgress or at least test generic boundaries. (Something similar might be said for the philosophical poet or poetic philosopher Nietzsche.) But there is, almost classically, a third part to the story.

Our own "backstories" almost ineluctably take at least three parts—"once I was X, then I thought Y [often with a sense of loss or change], so I became...[something other and more complex, but more real]." Thus, at the risk of reduction, the third part of Derrida's story:

> But it was no doubt much more complicated and overdetermined than thinking and saying it in a few words makes it seem now. At the same time, I believe that very rapidly literature was also the experience of a dissatisfaction or a lack, an impatience. If the philosophical question seemed at least as necessary to me, this is perhaps because I had the presentiment that there sometimes could be an innocence or irresponsibility, even an impotence, in literature. Not only can one say everything in literature without there being any consequences, I thought, no doubt naively, but at bottom the writer as such does not ask the question of the essence

of literature. Perhaps against the background of an impotence or inhibition faced with a literary writing I desired but always placed higher up than and further away from myself, I quickly got interested either in a form of literature which bore a question about literature, or else a philosophical type of activity which interrogated the relationship between speech and writing. Philosophy also seemed more political...,more capable of posing politically the question of literature with the political seriousness and consequentiality it requires. (39)

The third part almost explains, but perhaps it is just another part of the story. Perhaps we could say that in it Derrida speculates autobiographically to a willing and solicitous auditor (the interviewer Derek Attridge), trying to come to understand as a choice something that is difficult to present convincingly and purely *as* a choice. That is, in retrospect and as we all experience, it is difficult to decide between an interpretation of an action that casts it as gratuitous and one that casts it as overdetermined. Thus our own interpretations of our own acts are speculative ("Perhaps," Derrida says, "...I desired...") and waver between choice and fatedness.

In this autobiographical speculation there arises an interplay, not surprisingly in a binary form, between what is given and what is chosen, which enables Derrida to frame a traditional philosophical concern in the form of a paradox. On one hand, philosophy seems to bear the burden of being the tradition of responsibility, calling actors to given reasons for their actions, and thus to be a potent discourse. On the other, literature seems to allow for the possibility that one can "say everything" and therefore to break with both cultural context and reason, but only at the expense of a certain impotence in which, saying everything, literature negatives itself in its own freedom and possibility. The call to responsibility is then framed neither as a call to reasoning from first principles and logical necessity nor as a call to gratuitous invention, but as what will appear sometimes in his writing as under the sign of a paradox as a "calculated risk," which is to say neither a calculation nor a risk, or (perhaps later and more properly) under the sign of "faith":

> The freedom to say anything is a very powerful political weapon, but one which might immediately let itself be neutralized as a fiction. This revolutionary power can become very conservative. The writer can just as well be held to be irresponsible. He can, I'd even say that he must sometimes demand a certain

irresponsibility, at least as regards ideological powers...., which try to call him back to extremely determinate responsibilities before socio-political or ideological bodies. This duty of irresponsibility, or refusing to reply for one's thought or writing to constituted powers, is perhaps the highest form of responsibility. To whom, to what? That's the whole question of the future or the event promised by or to such an experience, what I was just calling the democracy to come. Not the democracy of tomorrow, not a future democracy which will be present tomorrow but one whose concept is linked to the to-come [*a venir*, cf. *avenir*, future], to the experience of a promise engaged, that is always an endless promise. (38)

This is a powerful reconfiguration and itself a rupture with philosophy as an attempt to discover what is—meaning, what is already given— and what one's responsibilities are to what is given, and a turning toward what is not already constructed and given. It is allied to the thought and figure of the "monstrous birth" imagined at the end of "Structure, Sign, and Play" (265) continually re-figured throughout Derrida's writing. It has no assurance or certitude or "perception" of right, and perhaps it alludes darkly and peculiarly to one of the darkest and most peculiar foundational texts not of philosophy but of the tradition of faith in the West—a tradition that exists alongside, within, and counter to philosophy as the text of reason and responsibility, to variations of which Derrida will return explicitly in his later meditations on the Abrahamic tradition and its religious derivatives:

> After these things, God tested Abraham. He said to him, "Abraham!" And he said "Here I am." He said, "Take your son, your only son Isaac, whom you love, and go to the land of Moriah, and offer him there as a burnt offering on one of the mountains that I shall show you." So Abraham rose early in the morning, saddled his donkey, and took two of his young men with him, and his son Isaac; he cut the wood for the burnt offering, and set out and went to the place in the distance that God had shown him....When they came to the place that God had shown him, Abraham built a small altar there and laid the wood in order. He bound his son Isaac, and laid him on the altar, on top of the wood. Then Abraham reached out his hand and took the knife to kill his son. But the angel of the Lord called to him from heaven, and said, "Abraham, Abraham!" And he said, "Here I am." He said, "Do not lay your hand on the boy or do anything to him; for now I

26

know that you fear God, since you have not withheld your son, your only son, from me." And Abraham looked up and saw a ram, caught in the thicket by its horns. Abraham went and took the ram and offered it up as a burnt offering instead of his son. So Abraham called that place "The Lord will provide"; as it is said to this day, "On the mount of the Lord it shall be provided." (Genesis 22. 1-3, 9-14)

What is the responsibility of irresponsibility? "To whom, to what?" Derrida does not of course invoke a theistic concept of God in his writing, and insists in pointing to his own "(likely) atheism," which is to say his lack of belief in a personal God. Nevertheless, he remains in alliance with this tradition, which is one that figures "the experience of a promise engaged, that is always an endless promise" ("This Strange Institution...." 38).

For Derrida, the story of Abraham is symbolic of a release from the calculation of reward:

> It is finally in renouncing life, the life of his son that one has every reason to think is more precious than his own, that Abraham gains or wins. He risks winning; more precisely, having renounced winning, expecting neither response nor recompense, expecting nothing that can be given back to him, nothing that will come back to him..., he sees that God gives back to him, in the instant of absolute renunciation, the very thing that he had already, in the same instant, decided to sacrifice. It is given back to him because he renounced calculation. Demystifiers of this superior or sovereign calculation that consists in no more calculating might say he played his cards well. Through the law of the father economy reappropriates the *an*economy of the gift as a gift of life or, what amounts to the same thing, a gift of death. (*The Gift of Death* 96-97)

Asking "on what condition is responsibility possible?," Derrida replies that it is on the condition that goodness forget itself, so that "goodness exist[s] beyond all calculation,"

> On the condition that goodness forget itself, that the movement be a movement of the gift that renounces itself, hence a movement of infinite love. Only infinite love can renounce itself and, in order to become finite, become incarnated in order to love the other, to love the other as a finite other. This gift of infinite love comes

from someone and is addressed to someone; responsibility demands irreplaceable singularity. Yet only death or rather the apprehension of death can give this irreplaceability, and it is only on the basis of it that one can speak of a responsible subject, of the soul as conscience of self, of myself, etc. (50-51)

This seems of course to be an explication of the narrative logic by which the sacrifice of Abraham and Isaac (both, for Abraham is, on this reading, sacrificing himself) is said to prefigure the idea of the sacrifice of Christ and of God in Christ, and to give a reason why death came into the world not as a hideous thing but as that which makes love possible—by making each person unique, finite, non-fungible and irreplaceable to whomever that one is open—and therefore makes "life" (not just motility and reproduction but consciousness and meaning) possible.

The issue for anyone who wants to answer what model of philosopher Derrida might correspond to, however, is whether this is "philosophy" in the typical sense that tradition accepts it, or remains outside philosophy and religion as well, for the interpretation does not include precisely those elements of Christianity or other religions that require a belief in a transcendent *and* personal God (God as Being; God as a being) and that assures one that death is only a transition between modalities of being. One has every reason to believe that Derrida does *not* say this.

Therefore, the shape of his narrative appears to imply the tri-partite form of a soteriological narrative or theodicy (a narrative of salvation or restitution that moves from being to a transitional moment of non-being and loss and thence to a return to being) while not participating in what Derrida critiques as "onto-theology." His reason for not doing so seems to be this: The history of either philosophy or theology cannot make sense of itself without a radical assertion of human freedom—which means an interplay of responsibility and irresponsibility oriented toward the other—that would be denied if the relationship to the other were subject to a simple economy of exchange, and if the relationship to the "wholly other" (which for Derrida is "any other" ["tout autre est tout autre" or "every other (one) is every (bit) other" *The Gift of Death* 82) were pre-determined in its outcome by a closed economy or endlessly repetitive exchange of the same. This is as much as to say, indeed, that love and goodness, in order to be incarnate must be transcendent (as, for instance, the Christian tradition would say) and not depend on mere appetite for satisfaction. In fact, they must depend on dissatisfaction, and a desire beyond that which can be matched or meted out—and be incalculable.

Almost—Western philosophy has almost said as much in moments such as the institution of the Kantian "categorical imperative" (so to do only that which in relevant aspects one can consistently will to be done as a universal law), which denotes a sphere of rational freedom and of freedom in and through rationality. But what is rational in Abraham's action of sacrifice, or in the Christian narrative, of which Paul says "God chose what is foolish in the world to shame the wise" (1 Corinthians 1.27a)?

Derrida remains committed to the idea of transcendence at the same time that he appears not to endorse the totalization of that transcendence in Being but remains oriented toward what he calls the "to-come" or the something that has not arrived, and is not now and not yet:

> What would be a path without aporia? Would there be a way [voie] wihout what clears the way there where the way is not opened, whether it is blocked or still buried in the nonway? I cannot think the notion of the way without the necessity of deciding there where the decision seems impossible. Nor can I think the decision and thus the responsibility there where the decision is already possible and programmable. And would one speak, could one only speak of this thing? Would there be a voice [voix] for that? A name? (*On the Name* 83)

This of course harks back to and re-opens a tradition in which the naming of God and the attempt to speak of God in finite terms, even the terms of "Being," are limitations upon the possibility both of the transcendent other and of the finite other—and so it challenges and critiques the rational and rationalizing approach of philosophy and of religion that thinks in terms of the calculable. It also allows that there is something meaningful in the halted, confused process of history which will shake the foundations of what one thinks is there, and perhaps open the way to what is not, which is figured in biblical tropes— especially that of *metanoia*, or the turning out of the way in which one has been travelling on a road of decline and into another way, undiscovered and not calculated upon.

**Open Ending II**

To conclude these introductory chapters and to attempt to put Derrida into the form of a resume of life and thought, we might briefly return to Geoffrey Bennington's statement that "Derrida does not 'do' philosophy, but 'reads' philosophy." What does this mean? For one thing, it is a rare thing for Derrida to say that anything except misconstructions of his own statements are not "true." No matter what the text, he takes a scholar's and an interpreter's stance toward it, and does not so much argue with or against it as he does inquire into and interrogate it. This includes re-reading the peculiar passages in Plato's "Timaeus" on *khora* (in the essay "Khora" [*On the Name* 87-127]) as well as Matthew 6 and Leviticus 19 (in "Tout Autre est Tout Autre" [*The Gift of Death* 97-109]) in as searching a reading as one can imagine being offered. It also means a generous and searching inclusiveness, perhaps even to the point of folly or irresponsibility, that does not seek the programmable and the already possible, but something new and other in what seems old and the same. Instead, he teaches where you would not expect to be taught something new and challenges one to consider what one had already thought to discard as marginal to the main theme, not as though it were the center, exactly, but at least as though it were a salient "place of concentration" (Bernasconi 99) of thought from which to begin to question.

# Chapter 3
## Phenomenology and Language:
## Continental Encounters

## I: Reading Husserl

> We must place ourselves above this whole life and all this cultural tradition and, by radical sense-investigations, seek for ourselves singly and in common the ultimate possibilities and necessities, on the basis of which we can take our position toward actualities in judging, valuing, and acting.—Edmund Husserl, *Formal and Transcendental Logic* (5-6)

Edmund Husserl (1859-1938) was a seminal "German" philosopher (born in what is now the Czech Republic) who was educated as a mathematician and turned to "philosophy" in the process of answering psychologistic accounts of number and mathematics—accounts that would equate number (for instance) merely with mental states. The significance of Husserl's work is that it affirms idealities or transcendentals while appearing to restrict itself merely to the observation of what he calls "sense data" and to avoid metaphysical presuppositions. His work can be seen as an extension of the Cartesian tradition: Beginning from the observation of phenomena presented to the mind (cogitatans, things thought), he attempts to establish the activity of thinking (cogito) in a self (ego), and develop a general idea of mind (in which we know each other and communicate) and a concept of ideality, in which the products of human culture and creativity have their final reality or disposition.

His significance for Derrida is that, as a precursor to elder contemporary philosophers such as Heidegger and Sartre (the existentialist philosopher who was a formidable public presence in France during Derrida's school years), Husserl had articulated a methodology called phenomenology and set out the basic problems of method and themes each would, in part, address. Further, he attempted to do so—or claimed to attempt to do so—without first assuming that things in the world were real or unreal in any particular way.

Neither Husserl nor Derrida is easily "read," and our project here is necessarily limited because we are attempting to explain and distill in a very few pages something that depends upon elaboration and successive movements of thought. But we can begin by observing something unique about Husserl in order to begin to explore something that is unique about Derrida: For Derrida's writing and thought gain from his encounters with other writers, and this is most particularly so of his encounter with Husserl. (See, however, John P. Leavey's query on the place of Husserl in Derrida's development ["coda" 184-185].) It is an encounter in which, among other things, Derrida develops a vocabulary (never finally settled into a set of systematic definitions or axioms) and initially defines some central problems and characteristic methods of his own inquiries. (Almost all of Derrida's writing takes the form of commentary, and almost all of it therefore both incorporates and works upon a given text. Only in a few cases, does Derrida *argue* against a philosopher with whom he disagrees; and then, it is principally against those whom he would say misconstrue his own writing. It is a characteristic complaint of philosophers against Derrida is that he avoids or resists argumentation at the same time that he is deliberately provocative.)

What kinds of problems does Husserl pose, that Derrida initially takes up, that are productive for us to understand and attempt to work through ourselves?

To begin with, there is the idea of "transcendental phenomenology," for which the epigraph to this chapter can be taken as a first gesture toward definition. To attempt to "place ourselves above this whole life and all this cultural tradition" is clearly enough to suggest a movement toward transcendence and a God's-eye-view of things, which would also imply an authentic center of judgment and perception. It is almost identical to what we would take today to be a philosophical attitude traditionally conceived, as one attempts to get at the meaning of whatever content of thought one wishes to understand

Phenomenology and Language
without simply and arbitrarily importing some other content as the basis of judgment. (In this, it has some relation to the methodologies of structuralism.) It is a strategy of mediating difference and reducing it to unity. (So Husserl maintained, in the tradition of Aristotle in *De Anima*, III, 4, where he defines what we would translate as, think of as, "thinking.") It does not reject "this whole life and all this cultural tradition," but radically seeks a position—an uninfluenced position, one might say—from which first to gain understanding and then to render judgment. It implies suspending or calling into question merely conventional categories of thought, not necessarily to destroy them but at least to evaluate them. Such a movement is not new with Husserl. Indeed, one might call it another reinvention of the primary impulse of modern philosophical thinking to set aside what is merely said or experienced and to say or experience again, as though for the first time, but with conscious awareness of it as an object of thought, *what we say we think*. The movement is both repetitive and originary, as if repeating a transcendental formula we could identify in Ralph Waldo Emerson's famous allegation and question:

> Our age is retrospective. It builds the sepulchres of the fathers...The foregoing generations beheld God face to face; we, through their eyes. Why should not we also enjoy an original relation to the universe? ("Nature" 7)

That movement appears at first by this example to be oddly American and naïve, and so it has been taken to be. But in Husserl's tradition—the tradition in which such repetition at a point of origin rather than appeal to authority is founded for modern philosophy—it is Descartes who sounds the keynote:

> As for the usefulness to others of the communication of my thoughts, it could not be very great, inasmuch as I have not yet taken them so far that much does not need to be added to them before they could be applied in practice. And I think I can say without vanity that, if there is anyone capable of taking them to this point, it must be myself rather than any other; not that there may not be in the world many minds incomparably better than mine, but because *one cannot grasp a thing and make it one's own when it is learnt from another person, as when one discovers it oneself*. (Discourse 6, *Discourse on Method*: 84—italics added.)

If cultural tradition had tested out and found some things more profitable (intellectually, spiritually, morally) to say and think, why not trust "the fathers" (Emerson) and "the Schools" (Descartes) and accept their mottoes as our own? Why seek an original perception rather than accept those precepts handed on for our benefit? (Why not?) If Emerson's intellectual egotism is overt, Descartes' is subtle. Descartes is also apparently systematic and logical, as well as sinuous and more than a little influenced by the scholasticism he opposes. ("Descartes," Derrida writes, "did not displace medieval theology" [*Of Spirit* 20].) Nevertheless, his insistence on thinking questions through from a position *de novo*, for oneself, is one that Husserl recapitulates.[5] Husserl's project can be seen as an attempt to re-found Descartes' method.

In another way, Husserl's attempted positioning can be read as a signal instance of modernity alienated from "this whole life and all this cultural tradition" because of the division everywhere evident, in Derrida's words, between "the theoretical and practical activity of...science in the very renown of its progress" and "[a] sense for life and the possibility of being related to *our* whole world" (*Edmund Husserl's "Origin"* 31). It is modern (and Western), for instance, in its confidence that "tradition" is to be subordinated to the "I" or "ego." For Husserl (as, implicitly, for Descartes), the products of earlier culture are "sedimented" in being handed on, having become artifacts rather than actions or lived entities. This sedimentation and the consequent need to re-think tradition is necessary because precepts are not perceptions, and because we cannot even understand the language of former generations unless we learn those languages from the angle of the utterer, unless we learn to speak them, or through them, *as though for the first time, as though thought and perception were determining the course of language rather than language determining thought*. This means apprehending the thought, meaning, behind the word. Already there is the implication that one will have to stand apart from language, as itself a part of "this cultural tradition," to achieve the goal stated here. [And how can one do that?]. Husserl will provide a case study in the complications that accrue if we only receive the products of "this whole life and all this cultural tradition." For to do so is somewhat like receiving reports of what life is like elsewhere, in all their partiality (the reports do not ensure that what was true then and there is true now and here) and believing them to be true here, also, by applying them.

---

[5] The "for oneself" here is problematic since "thinking" is both de-personalized and trans-personalized in this philosophical context. The "I" or "ego" under the conditions of transcendental phenomenology or of philosophical idealism quickly becomes "the" or any I or ego.

Moreover, it is like learning the moves of a game without learning the value of the moves within an encompassing theory of moves. Nor, what is most important, can we claim to learn from mere reports and applications how to discern what is true except by what he calls "radical sense-investigations."

Initially, this appears to be a restatement of a sort of empirical philosophy, already enacted and therefore not likely to yield new insight, and certainly not to yield something that could be called "transcendental." (Something is lost if we assume that "sense-investigations" refers only to what may be called, in a phrase that obscures the kind of judgment he calls for, the "external senses." See Aristrotle's classical distinction, cited above, between intellect and sense perception in *De Anima* 429.) These sense investigations seem linked to something else, however, which one might identify with Kant or some other "transcendental" philosopher, in seeking "the ultimate possibilities and necessities," meaning the domain and the limit of the domain, "on the basis of which we can take our position." But, unlike Kantian categories, these do not seem to be passively or implicitly given; rather, they need to be sought out and our position "taken." One could even say that, paradoxically, only by making ourselves absent from the scene as a kind of transcendental observer (collective, since the phrasing is plural) can we undertake the "sense-investigations" that will allow us to re-enter, as if initially or at the origin, the lived world of "this whole life and all this cultural tradition."

But, to make sense and to take a position "toward actualities in judging, valuing, and acting" seems to imply a recapitulation of the whole cultural tradition in the progress of sense-investigations, or else the project is just a piecemeal stitching together of whatever fortuitously presents itself (not unlike the anthropologist Levi-Strauss's idea of *bricolage*). So the proposition is daunting. It is worth noting that for Derrida (already in his encounter with Husserl, primarily articulated in the *Edmund Husserl's "Origin of Geometry": An Introduction* and in *Speech and Phenomena*, but always a part of his own project) a kind of method may be suggested in this kind of ambivalent, ambiguous, or in any case divided, participation in phenomena. The bracketing of the world and reduction of experience in the process of seeking "the ultimate possibilities and necessities" of any phenomena/experience of the kind adduced requires this division. One could, for instance, look forward from the moment when Derrida includes this quotation from *Formal and Transcendental Logic* as a footnote to his introduction to Husserl's "Origin of Geometry" to his analysis of acts seeing and of narrative construction in the photo-novel

35

*Right of Inspection* [*Droit de regards*] But one could also think that this is but one instance among many of a characteristic "double movement" or "double sense" that frustrates Derrida's critics who, perhaps, forget or do not admit that it is allied to a rigorous methodology.

## Origins
The orientation of much thinking in the nineteenth and twentieth centuries, but also much earlier in the modern period, especially in what are sometimes called "the human sciences," is toward a mode of causal explanation (analogous to some aspects of natural sciences) that attributes present states of affairs to the conjunction of prior states of affairs—in sociology, psychology, history, anthropology, and so on—without being able to give the kind of comprehensive account of the grounds of judgment (the criteria for truth) outside a sense of aptness or adequacy within an explanatory framework or story being told. These stories impose explanatory schemata on events but are unable to give an account of thought (or being) except as it is implicated in a causal chain of events. Much is referred to origins without the idea of origin being itself considered comprehensively. (See Geoffrey Bennington's succinct summary in *Interrupting Derrida* 19.) One could say, for instance, that a neophyte (like an apprentice to a craft) picks up a mode of explanation as one picks up a language and proceeds to apply (to speak) it, professionally, without having even much of a framework for "judging, valuing, and acting" except a generalized intuition and models of success and failure of a very limited sort within the profession. Nor can one well arbitrate between competing "theories" (i.e., modes of explanation). Curiosity alone would lead us to inquire about what is left over, unexplained, repressed, or simply forgotten in the rush toward explanation. But there is more. Explanations rise to fill a vacuum, a place in which you or I find ourselves and the objects of our presumed consciousness without explanation, to stipulate an origin (usually empirical) of our belief or being and acting. Besides the engaging formal (purely formal) challenge of the encounter with a philosopher such as Husserl—because one happens upon his writing and spends time with it—there are questions embedded in his writing that call for a response. What are the bases of judging, valuing, and acting? How can I choose among the theories and methods handed on to me? How can I determine their necessity?

## Timelessness and Existence
What is the "origin" of a timeless truth (uninfluenced or unmotivated), not in the sense of precepts or theories approximately

36

true (e.g., useful predictions) but in the sense of those that do not depend upon empirical verification ("sense experience" as a causal phenomena) and are necessarily true? That is, how do we discern novel apodictic truths (truths both necessary and absolute), those that appear not to depend on a historical sequence or context for their truth? Take geometry. What is the phenomenology of a geometrical thought that is always true (the Pythagorean theorem, for instance), that exists apart from its possible "origin" as an empirical generalization (and cannot be falsified by the appearance of new evidence), and of the signs in (by) which it is expressed? What is its origin? Can the history of geometry explain geometry? [Aside: The trail of signs establishing a discipline must be read in a later context and cannot return us to a time when they were not and the thought identified with them was not, but while we can imagine when the sign was not we cannot equally imagine when the truth of the apodictic truth was not. How does it come into existence? Where does it come from?] Can we seriously think that the "truth" of geometry depends upon its historical unfolding (for instance, the force of its usefulness)? What, then, would validate it as true? How can what we learn from an inquiry into geometry inform us of the nature of signs, not as a medium of communication but as a medium of thought, even of a thought which is separable from its expression and held to be true apart from any medium of expression? By definition an empirical history or anthropology of geometry can only deal with its appearances—texts and empirical evidence—and demarcate its inception at some relatively arbitrary moment—arbitrary because we are required already to define its inception by resemblance to a writing that comes after and is verbally identified and proscribed or limited by the definition.

If all I think is referable back to a set of circumstances that set it in motion (Hobbes [in *Leviathan*] et al) and a causal chain, what grounds are there for judging and valuing that provide for a choice of action that are not simply other chains set in motion equally accidentally? What other than, for instance, pleasure or whim would commit me to an ethical action, and what distinguishes it as ethical? If there is something apart from the causal chain of circumstance, what is it and in what space does it exist (if it "exists" in a "space")? This is the problem posed by the mathematical object in Derrida's encounter with Husserl:

The mathematical object seems to be the privileged example and most permanent thread guiding Husserl's reflection. This is because the mathematical object is *ideal*. Its being is thoroughly

37

transparent and exhausted by its phenomenality. Absolutely objective, i.e., totally rid of empirical subjectivity, it nevertheless is only what it appears to be. Therefore, it is always already reduced to its phenomenal sense, and its being is, from the outset, to be an object [*etre-objet*] for a pure consciousness. (*Husserl's "Origin"* 27)

In some sorts of philosophical worlds (Plato's, for instance, or Berkeley's or Spinoza's) ideality is not a problem as it is here: It is explained within the context of a world in which there are said to be spaces for all the objects in that world, even those that exist apart from "empirical subjectivity." But Husserl's philosophical world is one in which our knowledge is already reduced to what can be derived from "radical sense-investigations" and in which there is no presumptive appeal to anything other than sense-investigations, such as "the mind of God" despite the desire already noted for a God's-eye view of phenomena. As a consequence, it is a thoroughly historical world (knowledge is either constructed through the process of thinking or given as part of "all this cultural tradition" as the trace of other thinking activity, as in a text). As Husserl puts it in an essay of 1887:

Numbers are mental creations insofar as they form the result of activities exercised upon concrete contents; what these activities create, however, are not new and absolute contents which we would find again in space or in the "external world"; rather are they unique relation concepts which can only be produced again and again and which are in no way capable of being found somewhere ready-made. ("Concerning the Concept of Number," quoted in Biemel, "Decisive Phases" 150)

In other words, numbers require a signifying system that is not identical with any referents and apart from which they could never "exist." The concepts that are produced as a result of work upon "concrete contents" (counting, for instance) may result in the production of artifacts, such as notations of numbers, but the artifacts themselves are not the most *significant* thing produced and, in fact, are meaningful only if the "unique relation concepts [which they at best denote]...can...be produced again and again." One cannot stumble upon these concepts somewhere, as though they were artifacts, but they are historical in the sense that they come into being for consciousness through representations (writing in the broadest sense), but they are not identical to and do not replace "things" (e.g., "time" or "space"

38

considered quantitatively) that pre-exist them. At the same time, they are other and apart from the time and space of empirical experience and history, appearing and disappearing, as it were, and—what is more—are not identical with any positive manifestation or sign of their presence. Once produced, they do not lay around like unused tools but must be produced or activated "again and again" by the thinker. If one who knew nothing of numbers came across a collection of signs of numbers and relations between numbers (that is of "operations")—they would mean nothing because the signifiers are as arbitrary as any signifiers without knowledge of the relation concept which is produced. They depend upon tradition and yet through them tradition breaks with itself: When I produce this sign, I am signing originarily, even though I am physically repeating the sign given to me by tradition. At the same time, the truth-value of the representation I produce does not depend upon my individual comprehension of it. It must instead be true for consciousness in general, transcending my individual consciousness. If there were no generality of the concept of consciousness, there would be no truth-value at all, following this line of reasoning, which is consistent with most of Western philosophical discourse.

Thinking geometrically requires the reactivation of the possibility of geometry, for Husserl; but what is apodicticly true (the relation concept) is not altered factually and remains "factual" apart from any empirical determination not only for a particular individual subject but for any individual subject whatsoever. For those interested in the results of the institution of the fact (geometers, those doing geometry, for instance), or those who imagine the invention of geometry to be a revelation of truth rather than a founding of truth, the historicity of geometry is unremarkable and, as Derrida puts it, "[geometry's] normative value...is radically independent of its history" (*Husserl's "Origin"* 43). [Aside: Indeed, its normative value, if it is not to be just a question of my triangle versus your triangle, and one or the other's will to impose triangle-ness in the world, has to be independent. Now there's a problem, and one that troubles much public discourse regarding alternative and competing modes of explanation. What is the ground of objectivity on which we can agree if it is not contained in a particular discourse of truth that is not the transcendent Discourse of Truth?] But an inquiry into the founding of a tradition of truth is essential to the project of transcendental phenomenology, as itself an identification of how "we can take our position toward actualities in judging, valuing, and acting."

The method Husserl proposes he calls *Ruckfrage*, which Derrida translates into French as *question en retour*, and (with his own

39

translator) into English as *return inquiry.* For Husserl, the intention in historical inquiry regarding cultural inheritance is to overcome the "sedimentations" that accrue to thought in the process of iteration and, simply enough, when knowledge is handed on to me as precept or motto or a rote manner of doing things so that I am not actively thinking or not conscious in performing an activity under the aegis of the inheritance. ("De-sedimentation" is as near a synonym for "deconstruction" as Derrida offers [*Of Grammatology* 10].) An example, harking back to our first chapter, might be reading-as-glossing in which I read a text with a presumption that the interpretation of the passage that was handed on to me, as part of my inheritance, is somehow an actual reading, an encounter with the text that deploys my fullest consciousness of *what the passage may mean* in order *to determine as if for the first time what it does mean.* (For instance, if I learn the meaning of phrases in a language of which I am a non-native speaker by substituting for them the translations my teachers have given me.) Derrida explains:

> Like its German synonym, return inquiry (and *question en retour*) is marked by the postal and epistolary reference of communication from a distance. Like *Rückfrage*, return inquiry is asked on the basis of a first posting. From a received and already readable document, the possibility is offered me of asking again, and in return, about the primordial and final intention of what has been given to me by tradition. The latter, which is only mediacy itself and openness to telecommunication in general, is then, as Husserl says "open....to continued inquiry." (*Husserl's "Origin"* 158)

Or to quote directly from Husserl who, in this case, may be more accessible and fully explicit about his method than his commentator:

> Starting from what we know, from our geometry, or rather from the older handed-down forms (such as Euclidean geometry), there is an inquiry back into the submerged original beginnings as they must necessarily have been in their "primally establishing" function. This regressive inquiry unavoidably remains within the sphere of generalities, but...these are generalities which can be richly explicated, with prescribed possibilities of arriving at particular questions and self-evident claims as answers. The geometry which is ready-made, so to speak, from which the regressive inquiry begins, is a tradition. Our human existence

moves within innumerable traditions. The whole cultural world, in all its forms, exists through tradition. These forms have arisen as such not merely causally; we also know that already that tradition is precisely tradition, having arisen within our human space through human activity, i.e., spiritually, even *though we generally know nothing, or as good as nothing, of the particular provenance and of the spiritual source that brought it about* [my italics—SH]. And yet there lies in this lack of knowledge, everywhere and essentially, an implicit knowledge, which can thus also be made explicit, a knowledge of unassailable self-evidence. (*Husserl's "Origin"* 158; the translation here differs in the phrasing "regressive inquiry" for "Ruckfrage" from the Derrida/Leavey, trans., choice of "return inquiry.")

What looks like a possible project with respect to geometry, the ostensible focus of the work Derrida has chosen to encounter, looks less likely with respect to "the whole cultural world." Moreover, the traditional humanistic explanation—"arisen within our human space through human activity"—is given a dimension in the interjection "i.e., spiritually" that cannot be accounted for though it is said to remain "the source that brought it about [its proximate cause?—SH]." This meaning or sense is not available or accessible, is an anterior sense absent from our representations to ourselves of our now human, now "spiritual" activity. And, for Derrida, *nothing—no effort or intention—can return us to the origin, the perception, for the reason that there never was one determinable before the sign: the idea of origin or perception is an effect of the signifying system and not the other way around, however we may define that system.*

Husserl appears here to assert that what is covered over in other domains of human activity is as easily uncovered as the originary sense of geometry. It is only by assuming all the "forms" of culture—all cultural products—also participate in the production of "ideal objectivity." This assumption Husserl makes explicit:

All forms newly produced by someone on the basis of pregiven forms immediately take on the same objectivity. This is, we note, an "ideal" objectivity. It is proper to the whole class of spiritual products of the cultural world, to which not only all scientific constructions and the sciences themselves belong but also, for example, the constructions of fine literature.* [* Husserl continues in a footnote:] But the broadest conception of literature encompasses them all: that is, it belongs to their objective being

41

that they be linguistically expressed [in *essence*, works of literature are linguistic because we cannot conceive of a literature apart from linguistic expression—SH] and can be expressed again and again; or, more precisely, they have their objectivity, their existence for everyone, only as signification, as the meaning of speech [they are not pragmatically communicative acts; their meaning is identical with their form in the act of signification; and, in fact, as signification they can exist for us as meaning only as we come to have a perfect knowledge of the language in which they are expressed—SH]. This is true in a peculiar fashion in the case of the objective sciences: for them the difference between the original language of the work and its translation does not remove its identical accessibility or change it into an inauthentic, indirect accessibility. (*Husserl's "Origin"* 160)

To some readers this will seem as though it were a way of dismissing the metaphysical presuppositions of idealism by one door and inviting them back in again by another. And so it is once we understand that the point is to ground all knowledge in self-evidence (evidence presenting itself) open to sense-investigation, to re-activate the tradition of "Western metaphysics" from these grounds rather than to abolish it. But isn't the process circular? As Rudolf Bernet explains the relation of Derrida to Husserl:

In defining the nature of this circularity in the process of historical transmission Derrida advances beyond Husserl in so far as he considers negligence ("Introduction" 36), forgetfulness, and concealments (105), misunderstandings (82), in short betrayal as necessary ingredients in genuine transmission. However, this infidelity does not arise from some empirically grounded incapacity of our intellectual powers. It determines the essence of historical transmission [and readers may want to note that Derrida does not reject the use of a word like "essence" in this context—SH] and it could thus be described as ontological finitude. Thus transmission is at once preservation and loss, and the return inquiry is at once an exposure and a concealment of the origin. (Bernert 144; see also Christina Howells 23)

If Husserl's account becomes paradoxical, it is not accidentally but necessarily so (despite whatever intentions Husserl may have had not to be paradoxical). For that reason, as with all the philosophers whom Derrida reads in this way—that is, deconstructively—the point is not to

42

critique the individual philosopher but to identify paradoxical schemata of thought arising from the paradoxical nature of the sign again and again in attempts to found thinking on the metaphysics of presence and being.

Despite the appearance of a radical re-orientation in Husserl's comments on cultural products, we seem to be present at a re-investment or -investiture of the sort of reactionary idealism that underlies, for instance, T.S. Eliot's statements in "Tradition and the Individual Talent" and elsewhere (which owe a great deal to the influence of the idealism of F.H. Bradley, on whom Eliot wrote an undefended Harvard doctoral dissertation in 1915-16 [*Knowledge and Experience in the Philosophy of F.H. Bradley*, published verbatim in 1964]) which asserts as a normative value in literature the masterful relation of the author to the entire Western canon. It is an extraordinary leap that Husserl makes from geometry to literature, but one that is important to understand because Husserl's conception here has a legacy in literary theory (and because it marks an obvious point of division between Derrida and Husserl).

Husserl's notion of "pre-given forms" [what Derrida will come to identify as "writing" generally; that is, an iterable mark] as conferring an "'ideal' objectivity" suggests that literary works attain their cultural status first of all by entering into a realm of objectivity that is marked off from other linguistic activities (ordinary colloquial speaking),[6] an ideal realm in which the formality of the work precedes and determines the literariness of its expression. On such a view, what can be called "laws of genre" are not mere generalizations about what is likely to occur formally in a particular kind of literary work or as a result of the interaction of the medium with a particular set of artistic intentions. Nor is Husserl merely intending to describe an empirically-based effect of reading. Rather, "laws of genre" (i.e., "pre-given forms") are formal a priori requirements for the work being the kind of thing it is, that "kind" or "genre" being an ideality that exists apart from any particular instance or activation of it. Consequently, a canon of judgment regarding the value of a particular work, its place in and contribution to a cultural tradition, to culture generally, would necessarily give priority to the form of the work rather than to other possibly relevant aspects—

---

[6] This provides a good example of the logocentric ambivalence regarding speech. If it is more spontaneous than writing it is the less likely to be consider an enactment of pre-given forms which confer ideal objectivity; suggesting the need to think through more carefully the idea of ideal objectivity.

Phenomenology and Language
such as its felt appeal, the sort of ethical predisposition it might
highlight, and so on. Otherwise, it would not be "objective."

Most readers will be familiar with now somewhat dated attempts
to distinguish between "literature" and "propaganda," attempts that
typically have reference to this criterion of formal disinterestedness: A
novel with respect to its "novel-ness" and correspondence to a generic
ideal, on this view, is to be valued for having attained an ideal
objectivity by the integrity of the formal disposition of its parts more
than for its having spoken of or to a particular condition of humanity,
and quite apart from any simple sense of esthetic or ethical appeal.
(Husserl, of course, wrote at a time before one considered types of
propaganda as themselves significant cultural products that, oddly
enough, have their own claim to certain sorts of "'ideal' objectivity,"
constituting an autonomous world of values. That is, they propose
hermeneutic systems for the interpretation of the world, as advertising
does, rather than providing the impetus for thinking about or changing
the world.) Moreover, "pre-given forms" have their own ideal
objectivity, so that, for instance, a "plot" has an existence apart from its
embodiment within a particular reading experience or set of reading
experiences. In literary theory, such a tendency will give rise to
statements and counter-statements regarding the question of where
literary or hermeneutic "objectivity" resides and in what it inheres
(individual or transcendental consciousness, a quasi-transcendental
"space" of signification, etc.) and the relative role of the reader and the
text in constructing an apperception or or perception of a "pre-given"
form. (See, for instance, commentary on the "plot" of Henry Fielding's
novel *Tom Jones*, by David Goldknopf, John Preston, R.S. Crane, and
William Empson [Norton Critical Edition 702-893].) At stake (or in
play, *en jeu*) is a question regarding the priority of concerns that are
relevant first to the discernment and recommendation of preferred
cultural objects and second to the protocols of the reader's, any
reader's, experience in reading a literary work. Collaterally, the idea of
this "'ideal' objectivity" authorizes us to ask what constitutes
"literariness" or "literary language" as distinct from other sorts of
language (because all the aspects of a literary work are produced within
a tradition of "pregiven form," this predetermination would be no less
characteristic of what criticism calls the "diction" of the work). Finally,
and most importantly, this characterization would not only lead to
exclusivity of judgment, it would imply that such judgment is
authorized by an objectivity which has only now, and on the basis of an
historical outcropping of certain formal features in the vein of a
supposedly living tradition, been determined. Such a tradition would

44

Phenomenology and Language
not only *de facto* but *de jure* set itself off from and guard itself from the
incursion of any cultural other with its own alien "pregiven" forms.
And this would be true not just for discrete "works of literature" but for
a language, any language, itself: Its "pre-given forms" would be the
object toward which it aspires and which speakers would succeed or
fail to attain just as philosophers succeed or fail to attain clarity and
logic in expression.

For Derrida, as we have partly seen in previous chapters, the
principle of excluded middle ("either this or that") that underlies the
idea of genre and kind is problematic. For one thing, the mixing of
genres is not only possible but even quite normal, and the establishment
of genres is an historical phenomenon (which Husserl, too, admits) so
that the relation between phenomena and what is beyond phenomena
remains unanswered. (So too is the mixing of idioms and registers in
the speaking of language, and it is difficult to see the "pre-given forms"
of speech-acts as other than historical and conventional, although their
relative objectivity and alliance to what appears to be intuitive sense—
the kind of sense that emerges, for instance, from the collocation of
adjectives or subject-verb order (syntax)—seems immediate and not
conventional. Subjectively, speakers tend to believe that some things
both naturally and logically make sense and others do not.) Even at the
level of the spoken word or phrase or sentence, it is not only possible
but even quite normal for sense and meaning not to coincide; perhaps
they never do entirely coincide. For instance, how can one construe the
meaning of speech apart from the non-meaning of speech, its possible
loss of meaning and sense? How can speaking occur except in the
context, not merely of an ideal objectivity of sense which is [but then
how "ideal"?] being represented, but as a phenomenon that does not
speak to every possible human (and normally endowed, though this
"normality" is itself possible to interrogate) subject? Derrida offers the
example of a proposition that has "sense" without having "meaning"
(without pointing to a possible object) in the expression "The circle is a
square":[7]

---

[7] "The circle is a square" could of have meaning and refer to an object
in a particular context of utterance or frame of reference because it
could be an elliptical expression. The copula can elide a more complex
description: "Did you visit the circle in the center of town?" "The circle
is [now] a square." This does not negate but supports Derrida's
contention, since meaning and sense still diverge through the "poetic"
("non-literal") mechanism of elision. See Derrida's elaboration in
"Signature Event Context," *Limited Inc* 11-12.
45

It makes sense only insofar as its grammatical form tolerates the possibility of a relation with the object. The **efficiency** and the form of signs that do not obey these rules, that is, do not promise any knowledge, can be determined as nonsense (*Unsinn*) only if one has antecedently, and according to *the most traditional philosophical move* [my italics—SH],[8] defined sense in general on the basis of truth as objectivity. Otherwise, we would have to relegate to absolute nonsense all poetic language that transgresses the laws of this grammar of cognition and is irreducible to it. In the forms of non-discursive signification (music, non-literary arts generally), as well as in utterances such as "Abracadabra" or "Green is where," there are modes of sense which do not point to any possible objects. Husserl would not deny the signifying force of such formations: he would simply deny them the formal quality of being expressions endowed with *sense*, that is, of being logical, in the sense that they have a relation with an *object*. [Given the nature of the examples here, "object" would seem to mean a physical object, but this is not the case—SH.] All of which amounts to recognizing an initial limitation of sense to knowledge, of thought to objectivity, of language to reason. (*Speech and Phenomena* 99)

The case of an expression that has "sense" while not meeting a target of consciousness or object will from this point on in Derrida's writing be an important "place of concentration" (to use Bernasconi's phrase, "Politics Beyond Humanism" 99), since so much of "philosophy" is an attempt to rectify the ubiquitous errancy of language and, in Derrida's terms, to preserve (perhaps at whatever cost) the legacy of *logocentrism* (for which there cannot be a more direct or more common expression, lest we slip back into a language that is already sedimented with the language of being upon which we are trying to gain a perspective). If Derrida is original in his position or adds to our understanding (in the sense of opening up for us areas to which we are blind[ed]), his work depends on neologisms to displace the sedimentations of "ordinary language," which are the sedimentations of logocentrism. "The most traditional philosophical move"? Why so? Again, Descartes:

For it seems to me that my reasonings follow each other in such a way that, as the last are demonstrated by the first, which are their causes, the first are proved, reciprocally, by the last, which are

---

[8] See, passim, comments on Descartes' Discourse 6, quoted below.

their effects. And one must not imagine that in this matter I commit the fallacy which logicians call a circle, for, experience rendering most of these effects very certain, the causes from which I adduce them do not serve so much to prove as to explain them; on the contrary, it is the reality of the causes which is proved by the reality of the effects. (*Discourse on Method*, Discourse 6, 90)

What Descartes does not ever question is logic or reason, the formal template laid down to regulate thought that is at the same time taken to be thought regulating itself through language as a medium capable of arriving at truth—a relation of language to a transcendent (because nowhere evident and always not present) object. Else, why the notion of arriving, proving, etc.? So with Husserl. Which is not to deny the instrumentality of logic or reason, but to point to it as *instrumental*, to its *instrumentality*. It is philosophy that denies its instrumentality and insists on its (logic's or reason's) transcendent identification with being, so that "the last are demonstrated by the first." (Recall again the paradox of structure in the first chapter.)

### Is There a Genuinely *Philosophical* Problem Here?

In re-narrating the Western philosophical tradition, Hegel saw it as the history of a progressive series of formulations of fundamental but limited propositions or views[9] that led to similarly progressive (i.e., more inclusive and universal) impasses, each of which is surpassed by acts of re-definition and re-nomination, to arrive eventually at the realization of spirit and truth. At this point of arrival, the meaning of signs and their sense would be identical, object and perception would be one. Husserl attempts to identify a method (once again) to produce such an arrival, the arrival at the point where "we [a collective "we"— SH] can take our position toward actualities in judging, valuing, and acting." But a "position" is exactly that—a position—always situated and therefore, in one of the prime observations on which phenomenology is founded, always creating a perspective, a context, and an always limited horizon, and thus *difference*. Derrida does not deny the phenomenological implications of being situated, but instead emphasizes them, over against the totalizing and universalizing impulse of philosophy. But he does not simply deny this universalizing impulse

---

[9] Perhaps "predications" is more precise than either "propositions" or "views" here. The reader is invited to pass lightly over this overly condensed version of Hegel.

either, especially as it is a tendency within our world to bring together localized discourses and perspectives, traditions, languages, and to force us either to chose among them (to privilege one over the other) or to attempt to negotiate between them. Indeed, his chief philosophical insights have to do with the lack of perspicacity discoverable in philosophers who are insufficiently rigorous in their sense-investigations and of the sedimentations within tradition of their own discourses in pursuit of reason or generalizing theory. What *we* encounter in Derrida's encounter with Husserl is not so much an identification of a localized philosophical problem of the sort that can be worked upon and settled as it is the concatenation of philosophical problems that identify characteristic problems of and with philosophy. These problems do not go away. Rather, they themselves are sedimented and concatenated into each subsequent phase of traditional philosophy despite its strategies of re-nomination. Husserl does not fall far from Plato, as the apple does not fall far from the tree. His "ideal objectivities," though proceeding from "sense-investigations," take us to the horizons of our thought; but they also appear to suggest that they are the "source" of our thought in the way that Platonic ideas could be said to be the source of thought, its ground or origin.

It has been observed that it almost does not matter where Derrida lands in the history of philosophy. He discovers some similar operation of thought, some similar strategy of decision, that enables one to decide either/or, to cleave away associations in an attempt to identify proper names and a logic of sense—only to discover a secret elision or blind spot. Critics complain of repetitiveness, such that Husserl can and does stand for other philosophers and that what is proved of him is proved of all. What we miss in this approach is Derrida's own movement to open up again, with a generous hand, the play of signification that is often being foreclosed upon in the text at hand—Husserl's above, Plato's in the "Timaeus," or wherever. His rich explications of language, his shuttling between languages, his insistence on not translating certain vocabulary and thereby leaving the meaning of the text untranslated into a reductive equivalent, all attest to this generosity. Why bother with Husserl if he got it wrong? Partly, it is because he rigorously got it wrong and so demonstrated both a virtue and its effectual vice. (Rigor won't save you or signs absolutely from being disseminated, from becoming open to construction, misconstruction or deconstruction.) More generally, close attention to Husserl's writing or any other serious writing discloses to us those points in which we do seem to approach an intimation of transcendence even if we lose our way there.

48

# II: Reading Heidegger

> What would be a path without aporia?—Jacques Derrida, *On the Name* (83)

> [Questioning for Heidegger] is not a method in the sense that one uses it as a preliminary building up of a body of doctrine after tearing down earlier systems. No, for Heidegger questioning is a way or path of thinking each one must clear for himself with no certain destination in mind. It might be likened to making a first path on skis through new-fallen snow or clearing a way for oneself through dense forest growth. Questioning and thinking are not a means to an end; they are self-justifying. To think is to be *underway*, a favorite word of crucial importance to Heidegger. His general question remains constant, namely the relation of human being or human beings to Being as such; but the way changes frequently since he often gets onto bypaths and dead-ends. His persistence in holding to the question he has chosen to think about as well as his flexibility in approach to it are sources of admiration, even among the ranks of his detractors.—J. Glenn Gray, "Introduction" to Martin Heidegger, *What is Called Thinking?* (xiii)

It is a matter of frustration for some critics, already noted, that Derrida does not seem to come to a conclusion and give voice to a doctrine, unless it is the doctrine of a belief in a productive kind of displacement—of sense by meaning, the present by an undisclosed future (the monstrous mentioned at the end of "Structure, Sign, and Play"), democracy by democracy-to-come ("This Strange Institution" *Acts of Literature* 38)—and the openness of both texts and contexts to revision, re-writing, or re-inscription. And it is a bit peculiar that he seems continually to be going back to some text in order to move forward but never to arrive—going back even to texts which it would be hard to construe in some order of concern other than those imposed from without by requests to speak on or write on a particular author's work. Perhaps someone can explain the sequence, perhaps not. Perhaps it is fair to say, with the American philosopher Richard Rorty, that this double movement (backward-to-go-forward) is a late symptom of romanticism, perhaps not (see Rorty, "Remarks on Deconstruction and Pragmatism"). In any case, it appears motivated by an intention not to systematize, prioritize, or exclude texts from consideration. A random or imposed order is as good as any other, apparently, although the randomness is not itself sought out systematically. But perhaps too there is a consistency to Derrida's paths of returning to and reading texts (philosophical, quasi-philosophical, and literary) that are given to us by "all this cultural tradition" and deconstructing our previous readings of them (if you will, acknowledging canonical readings and then exposing the canonical to interrogation). Perhaps the intention is not to "place ourselves above" but *in* the complexity of tradition and writing. To what end?

If it were possible to say from the beginning where we are going, the activity of returning to prior cultural productions would only be to explain and to appropriate to a current discourse the discourse of the past—an activity that Derrida appears to view as the silencing of the disturbing voices of inherited texts resulting in what he expresses well as "nonknowing raised to a tranquil knowing, then exhibited as essential proposition" ("*Geschlecht* II: Heidegger's Hand" 173)—in other words, the kind of knowledge of scholastic inquiry, law, or administrative code. But what, alternatively, would knowing be? "Return inquiry" (*Ruckfrage*) is a trope Husserl used to express the activity of reactivating the tradition one inherits in order to test and confirm it by "sense investigations." The results of those investigations do seem to remain within the dominant (Platonic/Cartesian) tradition, and even simply to be a displacement or re-nomination of an idealist framework. Certainly it is remarkable that in analogizing from geometry to other cultural products, Husserl seems to turn evolving historical products into something like a static achievement of order and clarity—even though some of those products (the later writings of James Joyce, for instance) specifically challenge that vision and parody the idea that one can return to a sort of first speech and establish an ordered lineage from that speech to derived cultural tradition. Questioning back cannot travel a path to what lies beyond or behind the representation of speech because that implied objective is always beyond or behind in every movement backward.

Something like this is the view expressed by Martin Heidegger (like Husserl a "German philosopher," 1879-1976, and a junior colleague of Husserl at Freiburg). Heidegger attempts to distance himself from philosophy as an attempt to define or apprehend essences of "Being" that would enable one to reason from first principles (statements about Being) to logical conclusions about the nature of being or beings apart from our experience of finding ourselves already in the world. Here we are already thrown into things, already acting and speaking before we begin attempting to stand outside of our own acting and thinking, and always speaking through a particular language which is every bit as much a condition of "facticity" (constructing our possible choices) as any other circumstance. We can only think and speak in and through a particular language which we did not create, so that we are always thinking and speaking in a medium that is structured for us (historically) without its being mapped to the world in such a way that reveals the world without a point of view or from a *universal* point of view—though it may provide a simulacrum of such a view. Such an endeavor must be consider a break with the rationalist, realist, and idealist strands of what Derrida calls "Western metaphysics." Nevertheless, in seeking to shake loose from historical sedimentations, Heidegger is tied to a reverence for classical Greek as the language of first expression of Western philosophy (as well as to a more suspect and less respectable identification of German with Greek) which allies him with a sort of ethnocentrism challenged by Derrida in "Structure, Sign, and Play," *Monolingualism*, and elsewhere.

What if we cannot know ahead of time what truth or other objective we seek? How could we know if our language successfully maps the world not just in a way that reflects back to us what we (individually and collectively) project on the world, and in a way that is not just temporarily adequate but fundamentally so? What if the condition of our being in history—our "ontological finitude," if you will—is not to be able to know or predict or decide ahead of time—or a priori—what "being human" may mean? That is, what if the question "What does it mean to be human?" is simply the question that presents itself to human beings?

That question might take the form "What does it mean to question and therefore to think?" Specifically, what does it mean not to be a machine? What does it mean to be like and unlike other animals? What makes me like or unlike other human beings? How can I tell thinking from being impelled or compelled? What if I am both shaping and being shaped by the questions I am raising, the tentative answers I am giving to them, and the forms of language I am choosing (from those available to me) in the process of questioning and answering? If Husserl attempted to account for how timeless ideas come into history; Heidegger might be thought to question how we understand historicity—the human project of self- and cultural-creation—as beings already thrown into the process of self- and cultural creation, not standing apart from, but always and everywhere, in a favorite word, "underway [*Unterweg*]." The questions mentioned above are in their way Cartesian. In the "Discourse on Method" [Discourse 5], Descartes says that one may imagine a machine that can "emit words", but "not that it may arrange words in various ways to reply to the sense of

51

everything that is said in its presence"[74]; and so also a person, a human being, possesses reason as a "universal instrument which can serve on any occasion" and enable us to act, while it is "morally impossible" for a machine to be complex enough "to make it act in all occurrences of life in the same way as our reason makes us do"[74]. Heidegger's example is identifiable [within conventional assumptions about literal and figurative language] as more metaphorical:

> A cabinetmaker's apprentice, someone who is learning to build cabinets and the like, will serve as an example. His learning is not mere practice, to gain facility in the use of tools. Nor does he merely gain knowledge about the customary forms of the things he is to build. If he is to become a true cabinetmaker, he makes himself answer and respond above all to the different kinds of wood and to the shapes slumbering within the wood—to wood as it enters into man's dwelling with all the riches of its nature. In fact, this relatedness to wood is what maintains the whole craft. Without that relatedness, the craft will never be anything but empty busywork, any occupation with it will be determined exclusively by business concerns. Every handicraft, all human dealings are constantly in that danger. The writing of poetry is no more exempt from it than is thinking. (*What is Called Thinking?*, Part I, 1: 14-15)[10]

Thinking, we could paraphrase, is a relatedness and responsiveness to something in the world that is always in danger of losing itself in its own expertise and "facility." What is it in danger of losing? "Openness" might be one answer, defined as being "incline[d] toward what addresses itself to thought—and that is that which of itself gives food for thought" (17). But, in our historical situation, the "most thought-provoking thing for our thought-provoking time is that we are still not thinking" and

---

[10] Notice here, in relation to Husserl's implied criterion of literary value discussed above, another and different criterion. If Husserl implies a value in the renovation and reconstitution of literary tradition as tradition (like that of T.S. Eliot and other Anglo-American literary critics of his time), Heidegger implies a relation of the maker (*poesis*=to make)—writer or poet—to his or her materials—words—that would be analogous to the "relatedness to wood [that] maintains the whole craft" informed by but independently operative from mere tradition.

The reason is never exclusively or primarily that we men do not sufficiently reach out and turn toward what properly gives food for thought; the reason is that this most thought-provoking thing turns away from us, in fact has long since turned away from man. And what withdraws in this manner, keeps and develops its own incomparable nearness. (17)

Rather than being constituted in our tracing our way back through signs to original perception and being (the Husserlian trope), Heidegger suggests that thinking occurs when "we are drawing into what withdraws" and that Socrates "is the purest thinker of the West" because he remains in "the draft" of such withdrawing: "This is why he wrote nothing. For anyone who begins to write out of thoughtfulness must inevitably be like those people who seek refuge from any draft too strong for them" (17). Written signs (perhaps spoken ones as well?) seem then to be anathema to thought as the pursuit of that which withdraws; writing a kind of attempt to shut oneself up against the draft of—"Being" might be too precipitously introduced here, but perhaps we could say "whatever calls for response and relatedness." In any case, the purported subservience of linguistic and other signs to the commanding presence of consciousness is itself subverted by Heidegger's assertion that "Something which in itself, by its essential nature, is pointing, we call a sign. As he draws toward what withdraws, man is a sign. But since this sign points toward what draws away, it points, not so much at what draws away as into withdrawal. The sign stays without interpretation" (*What is Called Thinking?* 9-10).

Clearly, these metaphors and relations between them amount almost to paradox and represent an antithesis to what philosophy has often identified as thought (or to one aspect of what we commonly call thought[11]), namely, logic and ratiocination. And it is especially antithetical to the dominance in modern philosophy of focus on technique and problems of technique. However much a contemporary reading of Descartes may limit his use of the term "reason" to mere rationality (and however much Descartes' "reason" might be something more animated), Heidegger's "thought" performs an unexpected and

---

[11] "Thought" can have the sense both of a positive body of doctrine, as in "the life and thought of so and so," and of a vague tentativeness and openness, as in "lost in thought," as an expression of neighborliness with the inexpressible—an interesting example of a word divided against itself despite its sometimes being taken to refer, unambiguously, to a unified concept.

decisive turn toward something indefinable by literal, logical propositions.

Derrida's interest in Heidegger is variously expressed in essays and lectures that focus on Heidegger's process of thinking through what we could warily call the meaning or nature of relatedness and openness to something just beyond formulation, requiring metaphoric and paradoxical expression: So much so that it is difficult to determine where Derrida's attempts to explicate leave off (if they do) and where a general critique (if there is one) of Heidegger begins. (There is, in Derrida's writing, a running critique of Heidegger's relation to Nazism as Rector of Freiburg in 1933-34 and perhaps thereafter.) More so than with any other philosopher, Derrida seems in his approach to Heidegger to be extenuating and completing a discourse initiated by Heidegger. So our interest here is to see how Heidegger may operate in Derrida as a sort of influence that is not finally placed outside of the activity of deconstruction and inside the sphere of Western metaphysics but both within and without, as a kind of proto-text or text-of-having-once-thought-through for Derrida.

## Of Spirit

To gather this inquiry together with other thematic strands necessarily delimited by the scope of this book, we will focus on some of the questions that ideas of "spirit" (*Geist*) raise for both Derrida and Heidegger as Derrida meditates on the question in *Of Spirit: Heidegger and the Question*. A few pages back, we read a passage at length from Husserl in which he asserts that forms that are not generated merely causally (that is, by force of material action, as a rearrangement of material reality) have "arisen within our human space through human activity." He goes on to define this process as spiritual, and to qualify his statement, saying "even though we generally know nothing, or as good as nothing, of the particular spiritual provenance and of the spiritual source that brought it about." Yet he also claims here that "there lies in this lack of knowledge, everywhere and essentially, an implicit knowledge, which can thus be made explicit, a knowledge of unassailable self-evidence" (*Husserl's "Origin"* 158). If so, where and how? What do we mean by the language of spirituality, and do we mean (is it necessary to mean) one thing which can always be made explicit and brought forth in the light of self-evidence? The history of philosophy illustrates a bifurcated meaning of the phrase "the evidence of things not seen." In Descartes, for instance, effects are proof of their causes, though the causes are not seen; and, generally, visible representations of geometric figures are taken as evidence of thought

54

not seen, nowhere to be seen, and not identical to any particular representation. But the not-seen—the sense that there is a not-seen aspect of reality or being—is also itself an evidence; absence, as Derrida frequently points out, is taken to be a modality of presence, an evidence of presence that gives mute testimony to it. In Heidegger's conclusion to the first part of *What is Called Thinking?*, this paradox or inversion is brought forward (recalling Aristotle's *Metaphysics*, 2.1.993b): "The Being of beings is the most apparent; and yet, we normally do not see it—and if we do, only with difficulty" (110).

Here we find what we might call a mutual "place of concentration" for Heidegger and Derrida. Husserl writes as though the adverb "spiritually," though he confesses that we are "generally ignorant" of what it refers to, does have reference to what would philosophically be called a "substance"—a "something" which, even if we do not know its immediate qualities, is revealed in its effects. (Recall again Descartes' statement "as the last are demonstrated by the first, which are their causes, the first are proved, reciprocally, by the last, which are their effects" in Discourse 6.) Our lack of knowledge of the substance does not change its being, which is discoverable and which can manifest itself in "unassailable self-evidence" (i.e., the evidence of its effects).[12] And yet, curiously, it is not brought forth and demonstrated. On one hand, there seems to be an assertion that we all know what we mean when we say "spiritual" or "spirit," and that we all mean the same thing by virtue of referring to a simple substance or existing thing. On the other hand, there is a notable lack of demonstration of what we mean. Observing the assertion and the lack of demonstration together might—perhaps should—raise the question for us of how we are certain and whether our certainty is well-founded that by "spirit" we are referring to a substance the existence of which is self-evident, and then whether we can define that substance by its activity, manifestation, or presence. If "spirit" refers something identifiable apart from a set of accrued (in Husserl's terms, "sedimented") meanings conveyed by various metaphorical expressions—wind, fire, or what have you—this should be of interest to us. It should also be of interest to us whether spirituality connotes

---

[12] Again, the paradigmatic example (it would indeed, if true and real, be more than an example—it would be *that itself*) is the voice and word of God for Abraham, which stands outside of philosophy, for Abraham does not have to explore and examine what this voice is: It is self-evident and is of course for the Abrahamic religious tradition *the* self-evident "I am that I am."

unity or difference. In referring traditionally, and in almost all uses, to a substance that is transcendent, the discourse of spirit is of additional interest. "Spirit" as a transcendental (a mode or class of being to which entities could be ascribed as effects) would presuppose "being" which would be manifest through it, which would be the ground of "spirit" as a mode of being—e.g., in a possible series "physically," "mentally," "spiritually," etc. It would not just be the locus for a collection of semantic effects but, as it were, a real and unified ground of differentiated existence. (Although, here, in a concern for the "ground of existence," we come close to the problems of theology [how is the ground of existence existent?] and Derrida's meditations in *On the Name*.) If this were so, there would be some reason to say with Husserl—or at least to entertain the possibility—that "the whole cultural world" is not merely a collection of artifacts that reflect (endlessly) the variety of human sense experience (like refracting mirrors or echo chambers, as depicted for instance in Chapters 2 and 3 of Hobbes' *Leviathan*, Book I, or in Leibnizian monadology), but that it has a unity of being (in its being spiritual) transcending the specifics of time and place.

This would seem to reinstate the metaphysics that Derrida takes pains to question. Heidegger's reformulation of the Husserlian narrative (go back through signs, the expression, to reach the expressed in one's own perceptions) as a forward-seeking/creating of a path on which we are "underway" (go forward/outward toward that which recedes, which is being) complicates, though it does not abandon, the question of what it is in its generality that we would call thought and that we would seem to be seeking, a something also identified by the liminal or border-term "spirit" (and related terms, such as, in English, "ghost").

What is at stake for Heidegger, and then for Derrida, in the question of and the questioning of "spirit"? How is it related to "the question" and "man" as a "sign" (i.e., a question)?

The question of (questioning of) "spirit" brings together, as does the question of "being," a series of related problems of which we can examine several: (a) language and hermeneutics and/or translation; (b) gender, ethnicity, nationality, race, people, humanity; (c) religion. Briefly put, these related problems are:

**Language.** If there is some existing thing or mode of being accidentally called "spirit" in one language but (e.g.) "Geist" in another and (e.g.) "pneuma" in another, then: 1. Either the variations of meaning that occur in translation from language to language are *only* accidental and we may mean one thing in the

56

sense of referring to one thing of whatever order of generality, which would make translation highly feasible and only minimally problematic—and which would return us to the Aristotelian axiom that all men [sic] have the same ideas despite the different languages in which they express them [*De Interpretatione* 1, 16a]—or, one or more languages (natural or artificial) could enable a privileged access to truth and being; and, 2. Linguistic invention and difference, unless rigorously tied to empirical scientific discovery (e.g., the naming of newly discovered chemical elements, physical entities, or planets observed and the like) would serve only (as Locke said) to amuse or to deceive (*Essay Concerning Human Understanding*, III.X.34). But if different languages do map the world differently without there being a point of reference to contain and limit meaning (a set of ideas or idealities common to all speakers of all languages, or such a set to which one or more languages correspond more adequately), then translation (including interpretation) is both practically and conceptually complicated because each segment of discourse—from word to phrase to sentence, and so on—means by reference to the constellation of possible relations which are in principle beyond any single speaker's grasp. Every act of translation or interpretation (interpretation being a translation of meaning from context to context or from one level of generalization to another) would then be an act of (mis-)appropriation. It would and would not succeed in the presumed aim of a pure representation of the sense and meaning of the original utterance. It is not only a question of whether it is necessary to say that every translation or interpretation is in principle open to questioning and revision (of course it is, in the mundane sense that human agency can fail in translation and interpretation), but whether translation and interpretation is in principle possible in the sense of a pure apprehension of the presumed sense and meaning, the ideality, of the "original" utterance. This amounts to the radical question of whether it can be said that the meaning and sense of any text is fully self-evident, which would also mean that it is fully realized, present, and limited (because it could not be modified by changes of context). For Heidegger, this is a matter of "hiddenness." Just as our view of any phenomena presumes a point-of-view, and therefore a point-of-blindedness and undisclosedness, so with language. For Derrida, this is called under various names, most famously "differance," because linguistic acts never occur in a pure,

57

discrete present and never within an absolutely exhaustible frame of reference or context of utterance. [This does not mean, as he has been taken to say, that there is no meaning or sense in linguistic acts, only that these are not discoverable as ideally and immediately coincident with each other but always deferred and in the process of becoming with respect to different senses and meanings. See "Signature Event Context" 19, 21.]

**Gender, nation, race.** Foundationally idealist or realist thinking, which (to simplify) would hold that signs correspond to idealities or real existences, would also ascribe to culturally produced ideas of gender, nation, or race, a certain transcendence, so that terms such as masculine and feminine (despite even cultural differences in the social, associated traits of each) would refer to some category of likeness/sameness and difference that excludes any crossing over between them. Likewise, such discourse would (does) ascribe to nations and races identities that are either transcendental or, if you will, "quasi-transcendental" (functioning as such under limited conditions). Such thinking, of which we are all inheritors, would allow for instance purely verbal reasoning considerable non-verbal and non-linguistic authority. This is where variations of the term "spirit [*Geist, geistig, geistliche*]" become problematic for Heidegger and for Derrida. Readers of a certain age will recall the unthinking use of the term "zeitgeist," presumably meaning "spirit of the time" in pseudo-intellectual (or sociological) discussions of a generation or more ago (recently re-activated in Cultural Studies). For the empirically-minded (sociologists, for instance) this may mean a mutually influenced tendency of thinking at a given time and place, not far from a kind of degeneration of thought to reified repetition of formulas for thinking, in place of thinking. For others, it may mean the production and participation in an identity that is both localized and transcendent, whether that be the nation-thought of a nation such as Germany or the United States or some other country that claims its centrality to the development of human identity. Whether that identity is capable of being transformed from one state to another (for instance, from Germanic tribes to a proto-German identity, to German identity and thence, perhaps to a European identity and even human identity), it still has reference to a category of identity of which an individual *would essentially be an individual of that ideal class.* Moreover, it enables one to endorse the idea that members of a particular class or a class of people are further on the road toward some spiritual consummation identified with being and truth. We have seen, I think, how concerned Derrida is with the business of what he regards as the confusion of identification with identity—e.g.; so and so being essentially French or German rather than French-identified or German-identified (especially in *Monolingualism*) which is part of this essentialist mode of thinking. The easy and politically-correct manner of dealing with this of course is to go around in the world in quotation marks as "such-and-such-identified," though the apparent circumlocution of this phrasing makes such statements seem extraordinarily in-authentic—in which case, we must question what an authentic role or identification is. Why not just un-*Geist* ourselves? Because, classically, *Geist* seems to point to a differentiating quality of human beings. Derrida on Heidegger, loosely perhaps: "*Geist*...forms a part of the series of non-things, of what in general one claims to oppose to the thing. It is what in no way allows itself to be thingified. But so long as the Being [here representing the thinking of Heidegger—SH] of what one understands by thing is not ontologically clarified—not done, apparently, by Descartes and Husserl, or by anyone who might have recommended to us not to thingify the subject, soul, consciousness, spirit, person—these concepts remain problematic or dogmatic" (*Of Spirit* 16). Spirit, whatever it is or is not, marks the possibility not just of the production of the human as a kind of spider-web-like empirical, genetic construction but of the construction of the human as that which is able to question itself, its own being and the ground of its thought and action. But it is also capable, in being identified with one nation or tribe, of being stolen away from others and serving the ends of oppression rather than freedom.

**Religion.** "Spirit" of course is in the Western or Abrahamic theistic tradition of religion merely an attribute of the transcendent being of God (God-as-Being)—or, more properly speaking, it is such in the dominant tradition and retrospectively as an interpretation of the tradition—though it may be an attribute also, within the tradition, of other beings or kinds of beings. As such, it is, following the logic of (b) just mentioned, an aspect of "non-thing-ness" that has not been clarified for us "by Descartes or Husserl," and that remains "problematic or dogmatic." Within the performance the homo-/heterogeneous (Hebraic-Christian-

Islamic) tradition it is brought forth dogmatically or ritualistically, and problematized if at all only in homilies or in non-canonical writings, since scripture is taken to be the product not of rational *reflection* but of inspiration and direct insight. Elsewhere, in the "human sciences"—that is, those which on the model of natural sciences attempt to explain cultural phenomena empirically (basing knowledge on perception)—it is ascribed as a belief to certain states of affairs—social, political, psychological— typically as a kind of misnomer for the effect of empirical causes. For Derrida, the religious tradition has the virtue of presenting the problem to us; the empirically-oriented tradition of human sciences, whatever other virtues it may have, has the defect of suppressing, ignoring, or denying the non-thing-ness of the human—the "human" that it appears to hope to explain, but undertakes to explain only on the basis of its thing-ness. Why is this important? For Heidegger, in Derrida's reading, "what in no way allows itself to be thingified" is the characteristic that distinguishes human beings from stones and animals. Non-thing- ness would be precisely that which would make the human heterogeneous to origin (so that an origin, as for instance an ethnic origin, is always ascribed—claimed or re-claimed or renounced or subject to some decision and action of choice— however historically or empirically "true" it may be [e.g., genetically determined]) and, as well, that which brings the problem of good and evil—not merely creation and destruction— into the world as a phenomenon transcending the usual philosophical economies of "the good." Derrida's interest in economies (and an-economies, for instance, that of the gift) and the transgression or going-beyond economy of certain actions, such as is represented in Abraham's sacrifice of Isaac, has to do with the necessity of our understanding that something which is a "non-thing" appears in these moments of transgression or going beyond. Whether an act is good or evil, or good and evil, is a determination to be made of specific acts, such as Abraham's. But this specific act of Abraham can be read only as one or the other only by an extremely simple-minded reader. It is "monstrous" in the sense that it marks a space outside any schemata of good and evil or rational calculation of exchange (to recall again the trope from the ending of "Structure, Sign, and Play." Insofar as "religion" means a tradition that continues to present the problem of "the human" to the human "at the limits of reason alone" (Derrida and Vattimo 1, 14), where indeed daily we risk the

60

Phenomenology and Language
monstrous under the guise of one discourse or another, it remains
a vital tradition of whatever historical denomination. It identifies,
one could say, where that which recedes does recede.

If Derrida's writing on Heidegger in *Of Spirit: Heidegger and the
Question* represents a continuing interest in the question of the spirit, it
is not again for the purpose of synthesizing out of Heidegger (and/or
Husserl) or of revising Heidegger to create, a new philosophical
synthesis or re-alignment of terms within a philosophy of being. In fact,
it raises two important cautionary concerns. The first, and a
characteristic one for Derrida, is the concern with privileging any
particular language or languages as media for the access to "truth" or
"being" (68-72) and related varieties of ethnocentrism (see n1 to
Chapter VII, *Of Spirit* 120-122). The second concerns the confusion of
attempting a synthesis of something called the Western tradition (which
Heidegger also points out [see n5, Chapter X, *Of Spirit* 138-39]) or
transcendent progress of history or civilization or some other
transcendent process or entity, and the confusion of attempting to
retrace a genuine path of thinking (not simply a logical argument)
which one views retrospectively. For "thinking," if it is to be
distinguished from the ordering of arguments, is a process that takes
place forwardly and does not entirely anticipate its own course as
logical argumentation does: It is not programmable and the
configuration of the [dis]course of thought is different in retrospect
than it is in prospect.

Here, in repeating Derrida's words about his reading of
Heidegger, we might consider ourselves to have come to an opening for
our understanding of his (Derrida's) choice to use the metaphor of the
"path" to describe thinking. Looking backward, one can see that:

Heidegger's journey crosses, constitutes, or leaves certain strata
up until now scarcely visible, less massive, almost
imperceptible—for Martin Heidegger as much as for anyone. In
their rarity, precariousness, or very discretion, these strata appear
prominent after the event, to the extent that they restructure a
space. But they do this only by assigning new tasks to thought and
to reading. All the more so in that, in the example which concerns
us here, it is precisely a question of the very origin of
responsibility. (*Of Spirit* n5, 132)

Any activity of thinking that does not lead one to some sort of aporia or
a realization that the way has stopped or that one is at a loss to gain
one's bearings at a point of decision—any mode of thinking which is

61

transparent to itself both forward and backward—is one that simply recapitulates what is already thought and that represses the unthought that exists always alongside thought .

In his attempt to read the tradition of "all this cultural tradition," including discourse on the spirit, God, Being, and so on, from a position of radical un-knowing that incorporates with scholarly meticulousness a range of possible meanings and non-meanings but arrives at an aporia, a break in the path and a state of non-knowing, Derrida has sometimes been categorized along with practitioners of "negative theology." For negative theologians, talk of God and being is not simply metaphorical, allegorical, or symbolic, as it would be for most theologians historically by virtue of speaking of the transcendent in terms of the mundane; rather it is what one might call ironical or apophatic, speaking of that which *is not* in terms of that which *is*. For if God (as Being and spirit) is wholly transcendent (and not immanent), then God must be wholly other than all that is or exists.[13] This results in some peculiarly tinged readings of the New Testament, for instance, in which the truth of the scripture is preserved at the cost of its saying anything at all, and in which the obscurity of some of Jesus's parables becomes the obscurity of all because they all succeed in meaning by meaning precisely what they do not say. At its least successful, such a mode of interpretation and belief would read a passage like "no one can see the kingdom of God without being born from above" [John 3.3] as one in which Jesus is saying neither the same thing that the literal-minded Nicodemus takes him to say (suggesting the literal impossibility of second physical birth) nor a symbolic opposite (being born in or into a mode of Being beyond the physical, for instance). In effect, the meaning under the protocols of negative theology cannot be the communication of something known conceptually: "Born from above" (especially in the context of the 1st Century C.E. freshness of its utterance) is precisely a troping or turning against *whatever* conceptual expectation one might have.

While expressing his attraction to certain religious writers in various traditions of negative theology, such as Meister Eckhart, who speak only of God or the spirit by negation, Derrida denies the identification with negative theology that is ascribed to him. For him,

---

[13] Philosophically peculiar and scandalous (Derrida is not opposed to conceptual scandal), religious traditions that allow for the representation of God as immanent and transcendent, even in tropes that insist on the simultaneous absoluteness of each aspect, do not decide a priori between being and non-being.

every utterance is, prior to a determination of its grammatical-logical form as positive or negative (a relatively superficial aspect[14]), an act of affirmation. What opens a space for questioning is the question of what it is that is being affirmed, what it is that is affirming, and to whom. Again, to return to the story of Abraham and Isaac ("Here I am" Genesis 22.2), (something) does escape determination in the utterance, which depends upon the possibility of other utterances and predications endlessly to take its meaning, but which can never conclude with them all being gathered together in one meaning but is always deferring itself—in a promise deferred or a meaning (determination, closure) to come which never does come to conclude the sentence, verb, utterance that was begun.

One can only measure what one has developed tools to measure; observe what one has the senses or tools to observe; and one can only calculate what one has already rendered finite and calculable. That is the domain of perception. But one cannot decide a priori what is the measure of measure. Insofar as philosophy takes its project as the determination of what is possible within the boundaries of reason alone—that is, within what it has already described as the possibilities of being and meaning—it can succeed in making such determinations. But this is to inscribe thought within already achieved knowledge and boundaries of knowledge. It does not provide the opportunity for judging and valuing its own mode of proceeding except to correct a system with respect to itself. It is therefore neither truly critical nor truly open to discovery or creation, to the as-yet-un-thought on which thought feeds. It does not allow, in short, for the freeplay of the signifier which is always off center to its presumed target of consciousness. Perhaps we could say here that one purpose of Derrida's writing is not to do philosophy in this sense, but to read and engage with philosophy in order to restore this freeplay. Again, Geoffrey Bennington is helpful in deconstructing for us our own proscribed understanding of "reading" when he writes that:

> No text can make any particular reading of itself *necessary* (the text of laws is perhaps the clearest example here: laws attempt to exclude any reading other than the one "intended" by the legislator, to constrain reading to *only this one* reading, but show

---

[14] "Superficial" because grammatically and logically one can affirm a negation as well as negate an affirmation, at a surface level of meaning, without being able to tell what would count as a substantial or real negation. A negative statement is still the affirmation of a proposition.

up in the extraordinary textual efforts this involves the very impossibility of the task), but equally no text can open itself up to just any reading (no text is *absolutely indeterminate* with respect to its reading). Texts appeal to reading, *cry out for reading*, and not *just any* reading, but leave open an essential latitude or freedom which is just what constitutes reading as reading rather than passive decipherment. There would be no practice, and no institutions of reading [for instance, thère would be no tradition of psychoanalytic reading, no theology, etc.—SH], without this opening, and without the *remaining* open of this opening. (Hermeneutics is the dream of closing that opening.) (*Interrupting Derrida* 36)

Again, consider Derrida's reading with a will to restore the sense of wonder and resistance to ready interpretation of the story of Abraham and Isaac by taking it out of the hands of the interpreter who says, by reference to a certain hermeneutic code, that it is a story of the rational testing of faith [By whom? For what purpose?] and questioning it as it unfolds: Who or what is the God Abraham hears? In what sense of responsibility or goodness or malevolence and evil or lack of such does he go forward to kill Isaac? What does it mean to know, if one does know or does not know, the promise that is to come? Reading this story, often in another language and certainly in another cultural milieu than the one in which it was set down, we are perhaps faithful to the belief that someone intended to mean [but who?] something by it— someone who is not here to verifying that reading of an intention. And there seems to be no third party, except the authority of tradition, to whom we can appeal for arbitration. But what if our reading goes against tradition, as it must when another tradition intervenes to change our way of reading the story? And when does this tradition, as tradition, begin? How is it related to itself?

This story that is so foundational to the Judeo-Christian-Islamic tradition is also paradigmatic of the encounter with the transcendent— that economy of justice and love which resists formulation within the logic of being since, again, it inserts a sign of rupture and doubling that exceeds logic. The surrogate frees the subject from death. It is not the same as what it substitutes for (as a sign) and so it initiates a series of substitutions which are repetitions of difference rather than of the same. Simply put, the ram is not Isaac. Whatever act I choose, it is still not some yet other act and takes it meaning by a differential relation to other acts. That "meaning" therefore depends upon what is necessarily undisclosed—not "communicated"—and in principle always to be disclosed. It therefore implies a risk that is beyond the finite and calculable measures that are present and available to me. "Once I speak I am never and no longer myself, alone and unique" (*The Gift of Death* 60). But even after I have given myself over to language, which I cannot help having already done (so that I "am given over" as much as I "have given myself over"[15]), I still stand in a relation of difference that is different from any other—which is the point here in relation to a transcendental ego or consciousness. Provisionally, it is not that I am *the same as* every other I by virtue of the functioning of language in the naming of an *I*. The "I" puts me in play but not as the pawn of a finite, determinable being whose existence precedes and determines mine, does not require that I mean and be taken to mean only what I mean to say ("vouloir dire")—it opens, rather, the possibility of an engagement and relationship of response through language. It is the possibility and call of questioning things that are and promising "things that are not," to quote partially—perhaps to *graft*—from the First Letter of Paul to the Corinthians (1.26-31) that seems to figure, along with the story of Abraham, strongly in Derrida's discourse on spirit.

---

[15] The figure of "being given over" and "giving oneself over"—both active and passive repeats the structural doubleness of the oblation of Christ, being betrayed and giving himself over to death, and the ambiguity in Abraham's action, who both *acts* and *follows*.

65

# Chapter 4
## Speech Acts and Pragmatism:
## Anglo-American Interruptions

And it is this possibility on which I want to insist: the possibility of the disengagement and citational graft which belongs to the structure of every mark, spoken or written, and which constitutes every mark in writing before in writing before and outside of every horizon of semio-linguistic communication; in writing, which is to say in the possibility of its functioning being cut off, at a certain point, from its "original" desire-to-say-what-one-means [*vouloir dire*] and from its participation in a saturable and constraining context. Every sign, linguistic or non-linguistic, spoken or written (in the current sense of this opposition), in a small or large unit, can be *cited*, put between quotation marks; in doing so it can break with every given context, engendering an infinity of new contexts in a manner which is absolutely illimitable. This does not imply that the mark is valid outside of a context, but on the contrary that there are only contexts without any center or absolute anchorage [*ancrage*].—Derrida, "Signature Event Context" (12)

Man is a sign.—Heidegger, *What is Called Thinking?* (9)

If Husserl and Heidegger may stand for alternatives within a Continental European tradition of thought that still wishes to define and encompass philosophy as traditionally understood—as the pursuit of being and truth through language and signs, even if that revelation of total meaning is deferred—then they also point to the necessary incompleteness of that tradition. If they are not the last, they are among the last to attempt not only to define how words are used but to discover through language or "thought" the essence or self-evident being or nature of phenomena. They are, moreover, among the last of those who attempt to ground the knowledge of being in the certainty of perception in individual consciousness connected to a unity of being which is lost or obscured but which may be re-discovered.[16] For Derrida, Heidegger is exemplary as a philosopher who risks being lost and misled (and in acknowledging his quandary) rather than clinging either to empiricism and perception or to rationalism and deductive logic. In their respective phenomenologies, they continue, critically, the Cartesian tradition not to the end, because it has no end just as metaphysics has no end, but to its deliquescence. The tradition comes to an impasse, as does philosophy generally, in attempting to prove the assumption that a rigorous inquiry into signs—for Derrida, "writing" as an encompassing term—leads to the apprehension of an unequivocally transcendent (Being) wholly other than language or signs, as though they captured this presence rather than pointing to it as an always escaping non-presence. If there are, from the radical position that does not assert from the beginning a conceptual limit, an "infinity of new contexts," then the retrospective effort to discover a truth on which to anchor thought absolutely—an invariable certainty of Being—from which all other truths would flow seemlessly (without rupture, grafting, citation) is as the dream of summing everything up in one "book"—the Law, the Book of Names, the Domesday or Doomsday book.

Much as Derrida's reading of this Continental European tradition has led some to identify him with counter-traditions within it (such as extreme nominalism, nihilism, or negative theology), it has also led others to claim that he is allied with Anglo-American academic philosophical trends dominant in the latter part of the twentieth century—pragmatism and speech act theory (an offshoot of earlier "ordinary language philosophy" and yet earlier British common sense philosophy). These appear to avoid metaphysical speculation, at least of the idealist kind, although Derrida sees them also as simply or naively

---

[16] Briefly, again, Heidegger: "The Being of beings is the most apparent; and yet, we normally do not see it—and if we do, only with difficulty" (*What is Called Thinking?* Book One, X: 110). The paradox that what is most apparent is what we do not see is not an explanation but the axiom taken for granted as describing the constitution of the lived world, which remains to be questioned and *lived* in.

evading the problems of their own presuppositions. Conversely, representatives of these same philosophical tendencies see Derrida as being hyper-critical with respect to ordinary uses of language for legitimate ends (law, political organization) and unnecessarily concerned with metaphysics and transcendentals. One could say that if philosophers such as Husserl and Heidegger carry on a strictly philosophical tradition while attempting to begin without *metaphysical presuppositions*, the Anglo-American philosophers of concern here—J. L. Austin and John Searle (speech act theory) and Richard Rorty (pragmatism)—attempt in some sense attempt to *do without metaphysics at all*. For Derrida, that attempt is delusional at its worst (and Searle's blindness regarding Derrida suggests some serious shortcomings of insight) or simply not rigorous or thorough-going— could one say "philosophical"?—enough.

The metaphysics to be avoided Derrida of course calls the "metaphysics of presence," but this is his term and not that of the Anglo-American tradition. Early in the twentieth century, in Britain and the United States chiefly, the movement called "logical positivism" forms a kind of parallel to the evolution of phenomenology in continental philosophy. "Logical positivism" attempted to appeal directly to "experience"—as in the "sense experience" of empirical philosophers—rather than asserting the self-evident ideality of something like thoughts. (A "thought" in the most rudimentary sense in this philosophy is just a "picture.") Yet if it avoids the Cartesian reliance (whether avowed or only implied) on an already "metaphysical" inheritance—the existence of transcendentals—it is problematically naïve about something we might call "perception." It proposes (following a Kantian distinction of synthetic and analytic propositions) that there are meaningful singular descriptions to be made about things one may perceive in the environment (analyses typically begin with mundane statements such as "the cat is on the mat"), while any other order of statement (i.e., universal statements), in order to be meaningful, must either be analytic and "about" something knowable a priori (beforehand, as in tautologies such as "all triangles have three sides," or "every cause has an effect") or synthetic and "about" something knowable a posteriori (after the fact, such as, putatively, "all trees propagate themselves by seeds," or, more ambitiously, "every event has a cause"). And it seems to do so simply on the basis of our common sense assumptions. For the purposes of our exposition, we could say that this approach is linguistically naïve and simply not much interested in aspects of language other than the logical form of propositions—for instance, the semantic identification of "tree" or "tree-ness"—and of linguistic or semiotic mediation in general. In place of the richness of natural language, positivism attempts to found thought on an artificial calculus. As such, it is of relatively indifferent interest to Derrida.

What is of interest to Derrida is work that arose in part to remediate the lack of attentiveness in such philosophy to functions of language other than the constantive (that is, the descriptive) and that attempts to give an account of "how we mean" and what it may "mean to mean."

A focal point of concern is the matter of "context" (and, as in the epigraph above, "anchorage") and the philosophical problems of coordinating any particular, emergent event (linguistic or otherwise) in relation to aspects of context—including origin and end, rule, and intention—that in the sorts of analysis in question are said to "give it meaning." (For Derrida, for deconstruction, the emergent participates in creating its context and is not merely subordinate to supervening rules and determining intentions, but neither is it without such a context.) Linguistic events point up the problem of context by the familiar phenomena of misinterpretation when portions of discourse are displaced (quotation "out of context," being an example). How to define any event apart from its linguistic or other representation is of course a problem, since while phenomena may appear to us apart from obvious symbolic mediation, nothing we call "thought" or "meaning" is identifiable apart from such mediation. Outside of the operations of language or other symbolic mediation—"writing"—there is no thought or meaning. We do not for instance know geometrical figures except through the representations of such figures graphically or in mathematical formulae (both "writing" in this extended sense), even if an effect of this writing is to suggest the existence of such "idealities." (To return to Husserl and the example of geometry, in a very simplified sense, and to a common topic and procedure of philosophical reasoning, the comparison of all graphematic representations of triangles suggests that there is some triangle-ness that is not represented, that never can be represented, and hence is ideal.) And none of these makes sense or has meaning except within the conventions of the systems of representations (including defining axioms) that constitute the context for such thinking. Moreover, non-linguistic actions, such as a battalion of tanks travelling through the North African desert, have "meaning" only in the context of names, dates, texts of military orders and communications and other linguistic or semiotic data or predications. But as these data or predications are always in principle both limited (in point of view and content) and

69

revisable, any description of action that lacks attention to language and signifying systems is inadequate. The conventional opposition of language or discourse to action rests on predications already called into question.

Observation tells us that languages and pre-suppositions of culture are generally adequate to the circumstances of the culture in which they exist, and that cultures are open to local revision and change when new circumstances arise. Also, to some extent, differing contexts can co-exist and bridges can be built between them. Amish farmers can, for instance, co-exist with car dealerships and highways in an evolving society. But this is not philosophical in the sense of providing an uninfluenced position to "toward actualities in judging, valuing, and acting" (Husserl, *Formal and Transcendental Logic* 6); the suspension of evaluation, judgment and action cannot amount to the taking of a position. It is only a naturalistic description of how people live or may live. It leaves out of the story the fact that each takes its own context, including the existence of the other as subordinate within its worldview, as the whole context and is constantly elaborating a context in which its relative and local "truths" approximate higher, more universal, and timeless truths. When there is a conflict between contexts, between languages and ways of doing things, how are these to be adjudicated except by force?[17] Is it possible to find a way from description and re-description in the re-ordering of wayward descriptions within one context—as, for instance, when two people in conflict appeal to a power they both recognize and credit for the settlement of a property or labor dispute—to mediate between contexts. How far can one go in such mediation without the need for a third alternative which is not part of the original set of assumptions and propositions that make up the conflict. Is there, in a word, a context for contexts?

Again, Western philosophy has typically appealed to reason or rationality and the presumption of the logic of identity and opposition as the arbiter of conceptual conflict. Whatever was most consistent (non-contradictory) and most unified (identified with being) and—Derrida would add—most *legible* (most consistent with Western metaphysics) was taken as the next step toward the realization of a truth that was (mysteriously) lost in the origin of what was taken to be misunderstanding with respect to a previously existing truth (on the

---

[17] "Force" is in much of the Anglo-American philosophy to be discussed here customarily ascribed both to logic and to propositions (logic is itself a set of propositions). Whence does this "force" come?

70

naturalistic assumption of Aristotle that human beings have the same ideas which accidentally find different expression, or on other metaphysical or religious assumptions about truth as being something that resides outside ideas acquired from experience). But legibility (as well as audibility, one may add) does not depend, in Derrida's view, on the pre-existence of ideas to which signs are naturally connected, since a spoken or written language must be learned (no particular language is given to us as a consequence of having "ideas" as mental images or some such). To be a sign, a sign must point toward something without that something having been absolutely pre-determined. The signifying action is, one may say, an action seeking meaning and determination. It thrives on and is possible only because of the "free play of the signifier" and its ability to innovate without limit—unlike the ability of the Cartesian speaking machine, which could only innovate according to a pre-determined calculus.

Without making a pure distinction or suggesting an absolute opposition between the two, there is (in the first place) a concern to be adequately attentive to and informed about language and (in the second) a concern to be attentive to and informed about action. The first must be attentive to language as action; the second to action as linguistic, conventional, and semiological. In order of exposition, which could be reversed, these relate to a movement in the philosophy of language called "speech act theory" and to the movement in the philosophy of action called pragmatism.[18]

**Interruption I: Speech Acts**

It is now an old story: The preference for the spoken over the written utterance which Derrida claims to be a tenuous constant within the view of Western metaphysics bespeaks the presumption that the context of spoken utterance is more clearly specifiable than that of a written utterance. If you are speaking to me and I to you, we presumably share a context of utterance in which whatever is unstated is more or less present to our minds, and I can tell from your speech what your intentions are. How could my speech in the moment be anything other than what I intend to say, even if I genuinely intend to lie or dissemble? We both presumably know what we are talking about know each other, or at least know the ways in which we do and do not

---

[18] Both Derrida and speech act theory attempt to intervene in this imprecise division, but speech act theory supplies a theory of meaning that Derrida would (and does, correctly or incorrectly) regard as a re-introduction of metaphysics.

know each other. Or so the story goes, despite dramatic counter-examples and circumstances that should attenuate our confidence in merely spoken utterances, which of course depend upon those "citations" of "normal" speech acts that occur in drama and fiction (see, for instance, Derrida's essay on Shakespeare's *Romeo and Juliet*, "Aphorism Countertime" [*Acts of Literature* 414-433]). If things go wrong, the reasons are theoretically specifiable and we can distinguish between successful and unsuccessful communication, happy and unhappy performances of acts (e.g., marriages, baptisms) requiring both speech and the "presence" of the speakers. It might follow, then, that writing is a kind of attenuated speech, more susceptible to mischance through the misidentification of the context of utterance [but doesn't the act of writing create its own context of utterance whose implications are also specifiable?] and through the temporal lag by which written artifacts continue to exist after the original context or original intentions have altered. But, Derrida holds, all signifying practice, all *language*, is structurally or systematically open to this errancy by virtue of its citationality or iterability. A signature can be both identified and (therefore) falsified, despite its marking the point of the presumed convergence of speaking and writing—the point, that is, of self-presence.

[Am I not also equally present at the moment of writing? Is it not possible for me in the act of speaking to change my intentions? Is it not possible that in speaking I am less clear about my intentions—my intention, for instance, to promise and to make good on my promise—than I am in the reflective moment of writing?]

Derrida takes on what he sees as the promise and the incompleteness of speech act theory with an extensive *interruption* in mid-sentence, and long after the fact, of the seminal book-length essay of J.L. Austin, *How To Do Things with Words* ["still confining ourselves for simplicity to spoken utterance"] in his essay "Signature Event Context" (*Limited Inc* 1-23). His objection is, simply stated, that the imputed simplicity of speech is not simple at all. Like "Structure, Sign and Play in the Discourse of the Human Sciences," Derrida's "Signature Event Context" can be taken as a condensed public exposition of a critique elaborated, complicated, and rendered either more obliquely or more extensively in numerous places and occasions. At stake, again and decisively, is the distinction between "speech" and "writing" and the alleged privileging in Western philosophy of spoken utterance over writing.

Derrida's analysis in "Signature Event Context" begins with a critique of the common sense assumption that we can speak about

72

language through the use of apparently unified concepts such as "communication," an assumption undermined by the observation that all of our language about language depends upon borrowings from other semantic fields. "Communication," which might be taken axiomatically to define (identify and limit) the purpose of language, has a host of non-linguistic meanings that render it conceptually impure (that is, metaphorical) so that the philosophical (and, we might note, Cartesian) criterion of having clear and distinct ideas of concepts that we deploy in analysis is already compromised as we begin a discourse apparently based on common sense. But what, after all, is to be communicated and does it mean to communicate? Aside from the citation from Austin that is used as an epigraph to the essay, the Anglo-American tradition is interrupted here through an analysis, first of all, of the French philosopher Condillac's *Essay on the Origin of Human Knowledge*—a work in which Condillac explicitly sets out to "supplement" (to extend and to fill a gap in) Locke's *Essay Concerning Human Understanding* and its failure to accomplish a full explication of its own philosophy of language. Condillac attempts to demonstrate a genetic development of writing as a "supplement" to speech (and of speech as a supplement to "the language of action") which itself adds on to (for instance, by increasing the possibility of "communication" at a distance) and fills in a lack (for instance, of permanence) in speech. But this is at the cost of "presence" to the context of utterance and the self-presence of the speaker of an utterance and the idea or thing, the meaning, to be communicated. On Derrida's analysis, however, the fact that "every sign, whether in the 'language of action' [already tellingly bringing together two concepts otherwise treated as distinct—SH] or in articulated language...presupposes a certain absence (to be determined)" requires that "the absence within the field of writing will have to be of an original type [and not simply to consist in a matter of degree within the field of the same—SH] if one intends to grant any specificity whatsoever to the written sign" ("Signature" 7). If "the predicate thus introduced to characterize the absence peculiar and proper to writing were to find itself no less appropriate to every species of sign and of communication," however, "all the concepts to whose generality writing were subordinated...would appear to be non-critical, ill-formed, or destined, rather, to insure the authority and force of a certain historical discourse" [i.e., "Western metaphysics"—SH] ("Signature" 7). So, first, and somewhat obliquely, a philosophy of language that did not establish the existence of such a "peculiar and proper" absence, but just assumed it and—he does not say this yet but it is implicit following the epigraph—simply focused on speech as the

73

defining and proper medium of language and communication "for [the sake of] simplicity" would be insufficiently attentive to language and communication in general. Such a philosophy would assume that speech defines the common field of language, that its apparent features when considered by itself alone were the normative features of language, in relation to which the apparently unique features of other media, such as writing, would therefore appear to be aberrant or abnormal. And it is what he takes to be Austin's, and later John R. Searle's, assumptions about what is normal and not normal in language use that Derrida puts into play again.

In part, one can see an inheritance of phenomenology here, because phenomenology is a discipline of sorting out likenesses and differences among phenomena to arrive at what Husserl would call "idealities" but which we would more commonly call "concepts"—not just clearly and distinct ideas as simple sense impressions (phenomena to be evaluated) but the products of radical and rigorous "sense-investigations." What phenomenology most usefully points out, especially in Heidegger's investigations, is the non-obviousness of meaning, the sense that is un-disclosed in the obvious and the obviousness of the un-disclosed (i.e., Being). It encourages us in fact, in Heidegger's rendition, to attend to the borders and margins of the defining "path" of thought as a challenge to definition. This is anything but a denial that such paths exist—or that there are intentions, contexts, and so on—but a sort of strategy of displacement to reveal that the most obvious or most commonsensical is not necessarily universal or logically prior to any other.

"Citationality" or "iterability" appears to be an obvious feature that distinguishes "writing" from the normality of "speech." That is, a piece of writing can be taken out of one context and grafted into a new context, and whole discourses are communicable though received in the absence of the sender and sent in the absence the receiver, in ways that appear to be obviously distinct from speech. It is worth attending to Derrida's exposition of the written sign at length:

A written sign is proffered in the absence of the receiver. How to style this absence? One could say that at the moment when I am writing, the receiver may be absent from my field of present perception. But is not this absence merely a distant presence, one which is delayed or which, in one form or another, is idealized in its representation? This does not seem to be the case, or at least this distance, divergence, delay, this deferral [*differance*] must be capable of being carried to a certain absoluteness of absence if the

74

Speech Acts and Pragmatism
structure of writing, assuming that writing exists [i.e. that it is essentially different from speech—SH], is to constitute itself. It is at this point that the *differance* as writing could no longer (be) an (ontological) modification of presence. In order for my "written communication" to retain its function as writing, i.e., its readability, it must remain readable despite the absolute disappearance of any receiver, determined in general. My communication must be repeatable—iterable—in the absolute absence of any receiver or of any empirically determinable collectivity of receivers. Such iterability (*iter*, again, probably comes from *itara*, other in Sanskrit, and everything that follows can be read as the working out of the logic that ties repetition to alterity) structures the mark of writing itself, no matter what particular kind of writing is involved....A writing that is not structurally readable—iterable—beyond the death of the addressee would not be writing. (7)

To be what is, all writing must...be capable of functioning in the radical absence of every empirically determined receiver in general. And this absence is not a continuous modification of presence, it is a rupture in presence, the "death" or the possibility of the "death" of the receiver inscribed in the structure of the mark. (8)

Writing (and/or speech) would not be intelligible if it were tethered absolutely to the presence and desire to say (*vouloir dire*) of an individual subject, would not be writing (and/or speech), because it is exactly what is repeatable (iterable) that stands out against the background of the non-repeatable (non-iterable). It is other than either the speaker or the receiver.

Searle's response is to say that Derrida has, in a sense, overplayed his hand. (See, for instance, "Reiterating the Differences: A Reply to Derrida"; and "The World Turned Upside Down", *New York Review of Books* [October 27, 1983] rpt. in Madison, *Working Through Derrida*.[19]) According to Searle, it is merely that writing is more permanent than speech that makes for a relevant (and necessary) distinction. Intention must supply writing or speech with meaning in a

---

[19] "The World Turned Upside Down" was in fact a review of a book, *On Deconstruction*, by the American literary critic Jonathan Culler, which could be said in retrospect to be a premature assimilation of Derrida in the context of the inheritance of American "New Criticism."

Speech Acts and Pragmatism

determinable context. But Derrida has not denied either the relevance of intention or of context to canons of interpretation; he has, instead, pointed out that (1) the persistence or extinction of the reputed holder of an intention does not control or exhaust the meaning of any utterance and (2) that any form of words or other signs is capable of functioning in multiple contexts so that one cannot exhaust the possible meanings of an utterance by the stipulation of a particular context. It is always possible to be meaning more, less, and other than what we could be interpreted to intend. Otherwise, we should never need interpreters or canons. In short, he points up the naivete of trying to account for the functioning of language by reference to presumably normal or ordinary uses of language, which establish the "proper" functioning of language, as distinct from abnormal, "parasitic," and "non-serious" uses. Properness is not a property of words or utterances themselves. Searle writes that a "meaningful sentence is just a standing possibility of the corresponding (intentional) speech act," which assumes (1) that the interpretation of the "meaningful sentence" is already given (or else how could one identify the "corresponding speech act"?) and (2) that meaning is to be identified with the potential intention of a potential speaker, while writing is simply (as Aristotle or Condillac or Western philosophy generally would have it) the representation of speech, the meaning of which is self-evident (always, to potentially similar speakers of the same language). It is, in particular, a concern to correct the apparent belief that the meaning of speech is self-evident in context, gives evidence of itself, whereas writing in contrast is not and does not, that initiates Derrida's attempt to supplement Austin's gesture toward an approach to language that treats utterances as *acts*. No meaning is absolutely determined by and forever tethered to a presiding and persisting intention. A "sentence" or "utterance" is put in play, pointing to the possibility of meaning, but that meaning is never ontologically finalized by corresponding to an "intention" to which we have no independent access for the purposes of confirmation.

Derrida's attraction, in the first place, to the object of his critique is that Austin's investigations seemed to have promised an analysis that did not restrict meaning in language simply to "the transference or passage of a thought content" but included the possibility of "the communication of an original movement..., an operation and the production of an effect" ("Signature Event Context" 13) and the introduction of some movement that exceeds "semantic content that is already constituted and dominated by an orientation toward truth" (13-14). But, he complains, because of Austin's insistence (even if only for the sake "of simplicity") on focusing on and giving priority to spoken

76

utterance, he "blurs all the oppositions" in a "system of predicates" of "locution" that are revealed by attention to writing or what Derrida refers to as [the] *"graphematic in general"* (14). For instance, if it is taken (if it is our common notion) that written language can be cited or citational whereas spoken language is somehow original and authentic (self-authenticating) in performing certain acts, then we merely reinstate the old prejudices and divisions of writing and speech while failing to attend to relevant similarities. In short, Searle's description of a meaningful sentence is circular in just the same way that the preceding philosophical tradition keeps being circular: How could we "know" the meaning of a "corresponding speech act" [tied apparently to some intention and context] as the meaning of a written sentence if we did not already know the meaning of the written sentence in the field of possible meanings—including those that are "not normal"?

"Iterability" is a key to the deconstructive view that utterances as repetitions (of the same) are always different and differing from other instances (of the same). On first consideration, this might seem like a trivial observation except that, for Derrida, whether Western thought (including Saussure's structural linguistics and Levi Strauss's structural anthropology, as well as speech act theory) avows it or not, it always includes the view that speech acts or utterances are imperfect representations of some prior cognitive entity or ideality, such as but not limited to the "intention" behind "the corresponding (intentional) speech act." For Derrida, "intentions" are not meaningfully physical or metaphysical entities in a consciousness that presides over the production of discourse; they are effects of the signifying system from which one cannot infer directly any other operative entity or being, as to do so is simply, again, to posit or assume a cause related to an effect. Whatever empirical science may mean by "consciousness," equating it with certain biochemical states for instance, cannot be the same as these effects which are not reducible to a single thing or to thing-ness at all. But the contrary, idealistic, alternative is also not certainly established: the transcendental object can only be thought of as an effect of the signifying system. That I, Stephen Hahn, am an effect of identifications and predications, including the one that I may disappear as the one who signs as Stephen Hahn, does not warrant the belief that there corresponds to it a transcendent ideality. (It does not disprove it either, which allows for Derrida's extended encounter with religion, especially in his later writing [see among other texts, Derrida, *Adieu to Emmanuel Levinas*; Derrida and Vattimo, *Religion*; and Caputo, *The Prayers and Tears of Jacque Derrida: Religion without Religion*].)

**Interruption II: Pragmatism or Religion?**

Speech Act Theory does not differ far from a pragmatic theory of communication except that it introduces category of intentionality that appears to recapitulate the rationalist and idealist inheritance of Western philosophical thinking. This is not to say that Derrida denies the intuition of intention, any more than did David Hume (with whom he expresses a certain affinity), but that he denies that this intuition refers to a permanent or metaphysical entity. (See Hume's *A Treatise of Human Nature*, Book I, Part IV, Section VI: "Self or person is not any one impression, but that to which our several impressions and ideas are suppos'd to have reference. If any impression gives rise to the idea of the self, that impression must continue invariably the same, through the whole course of our lives; since self is supposed to exist invariably after that manner. But there is no impression constant and invariable," etc. 251). A consequence for a theory of action would be to say that persons are effects of the signifying systems and predications and identifications which are consequent to them (such as implied by Derrida's own biographical reflections) in which the self is, in effect, actively composed not only of choices or decisions referred to the identify implied by the proper name but also of those predications which it inherits. At the same time, this seems to leave out of play the possibility of an organizing political and social discourse that would transcend merely accidental or arbitrary identifications. "Iterability" with respect to purely linguistic phenomena is an aspect of the openness of all utterances and signification to re-contextualization; this would appear to leave all action open, in principle, to grafting and revision, and therefore to make action morally, ethically, and politically indeterminate—or only provisionally determinate. Lacking a grounding in universal "reason" by virtue of this openness, any and all historical conflicts would be resolvable only by force, justice would merely be the imposition of one localized "reason" or rationale over another, and one would not be far in theory from Hobbesian "war of every one against every one; in which case everyone is governed by his own reason" (*Leviathan* Part I, Chapter XIV, 4: 86).

On one hand, in attempting to find a path beyond this aporia, Derrida returns to the *ethos* of biblical religion and a reprise and questioning of values that seem to have provided a framework for the evolution of ideas of self and other—the value of hospitality, for instance, which welcomes the stranger. On the other, in placing himself in opposition to rationalist social theory—such as that of the theorist Jurgen Habermas who, in the words of Chantal Mouffe, wants "to find a viewpoint standing above politics from which one could guarantee

78

the superiority of democracy" ("Deconstruction, Pragmatism, and Democracy" 4; again recalling the language of Husserl's *Formal and Transcendental Logic* 5)—he seems implicitly by such opposition to occupy a place among pragmatists whose social views could be said to be re-inventions of Hobbes's pragmatic theory of civil society (basing the common good in individual and collective enlightened self-interest).

Against this possible identification of Derrida with pragmatism, Richard Rorty has argued that "deconstruction" has no positive value for social theory because, as Derrida practices it, is a merely "private" exercise in "self-fashioning" ("Remarks on Deconstruction and Pragmatism" 17) which, in seeking to avoid the supposed metaphysics of rationalism or naturalism, merely backs itself into a corner of irrelevance with respect to social or political theory of action.

Consider Derrida's choice of the story of Abraham as the paradigmatic or emblematic story of choice: How and in what way does this figure into a theory of action or politics? For is this not the type of story to which he alludes in the following critique of the certainty of political determinations (or other determinations of action)?

> Every time I hear someone say that "I have taken a decision," or "I have assumed my responsibilities," I am suspicious because if there is responsibility or decision one cannot determine them as such or have certainty or good conscience with regard to them. If I conduct myself particularly well with regard to someone, I know that it is to the detriment of an other; of one nation to the detriment of another nation, of one family to the detriment of another, of my friends to the detriment of other friends or non-friends, etc. This is the infinitude that inscribes itself within responsibility; otherwise there would be no ethical problems or decisions. And this is why undecidability is not a moment to be traversed and overcome. Conflicts of duty—and there is only duty in conflict—are interminable and even when I taken my decision and do something, undecidability is not at an end. I know that I have not done enough and it is in this way that morality continues, that history and politics continue....The relation to the other does not close itself off, and it is because of this that there is history and one tries to act politically. ("Remarks on Deconstruction and Pragmatism" 86-87)

Such an "infinitude," however, imposes its burden only on the condition that one consider all imperatives equally compelling in all

Speech Acts and Pragmatism
contexts—those involving my friends *and* my enemies, for instance. This is, of course, the point of several biblical injunctions, especially those of Matthew 5-7 (called "the Beatitudes"). These injunctions are not programmed or pre-decided according to the common law of property and exchange, at the same time that they do not alter that law ("Do not think that I come to abolish the law or the prophets" Matthew 5.17a). They do, however, mean that "the relation to the other does not close itself off" in the sense that one is not acquitted of responsibility by merely discharging a debt or following a command.

While such a logic or reason of which reason knows not—a reason that denies the primacy of the self in relation to the other and therefore the primacy of any single certainty of identity, such as that of the nation-state—clearly can accord with action in history and in the political arena broadly conceived, they are not the stuff of which cities and nations are made. They represent the *ethos* of one who stands outside of, not necessarily above, the city and the nation, though he may stand no-where and represent the "no-thing" that is "spirit"—stand in W.H. Auden's phrase "in the Kingdom of Anxiety" ("For the Time Being" [1944] 1513) which may be a good place to stand but which is not the place of determination on which the cities and states as defenses against anxiety are founded.

Representing an aggressively engaged, liberal, pragmatic politics that sometimes sounds like philosophical trade-unionism or syndicalism, Rorty casts Derrida as "romantically idealistic" ("Remarks" 13) though one has to say that the idealism ascribed is attitudinal rather than philosophical. One might find him speaking from a religious motive that has affinities with aspects of European literary and philosophical romanticism—difficult as these may be to specify exactly—but also one that echoes a prophetic biblical tradition without, in the end, signing on to the theology of the name that such a tradition implies (see, for instance, Ecclesiasticus or Sirach 44. 1-14).

# Chapter 5
## Aporia

How are we to make sense of the intuition that in some deep sense Derrida is constantly saying *the same*, while constantly saying new and surprising things and thematically valorizing the new and the surprising?—Geoffrey Bennington, *Interrupting Derrida* (194)

In what you call my books, what is first of all put into question is the unity of the book and the unity "book" considered as a perfect totality, with all the implications of such a concept.....Under these titles it is solely a question of a unique and differentiated textual "operation," if you will, whose unfinished movement assigns itself no absolute beginning, and which, though it is entirely consumed by the reading of other texts, in a certain fashion refers only to its own writing. We must adjust to conceiving the two ideas together. Therefore it would be impossible to provide a linear, deductive representation of these works that would correspond to some "logical order." Such an order is also in question, even if, I think, an entire phase or face of my texts conforms to its demands, at least by simulacrum, in order to inscribe it, in turn, into a composition that this order no longer governs. You know, in fact, that above all it is necessary to read and re-read those in whose wake I write, the "books" in whose margins and between whose lines I mark out and read a text simultaneously almost identical and entirely other, that I would even hesitate, for obvious reasons, to call fragmentary.—Jacques Derrida, *Positions* (3-4)

The preceding short chapters comprise something that itself could be called the simulacrum of a book as a short series of attempts at presenting Derrida to a reader whose interest is in an introduction to this elusive "subject." By their brevity and compression, they necessarily miss opportunities to explore implications of Derrida's writing and in fact renounce the opportunity to address some of the traditionally larger topics of interest to the same reader: What, for instance, does Derrida have to say about the inheritance—and preservation—of Marx after the trumpeted demise of something called Communism? Or about the inheritance—and preservation—of Freud in the wake of institutional psychoanalysis? These are implications one can explore elsewhere. But how to sum up what is central in a writer who has questioned thoroughly the notion of structures with centers, of organizations of thought and discourse called books (while writing some things that look like books and others that challenge the look of books), and....One could list analogous "operations" as mentioned above at some length. "Such an order [a 'logical order' authorizing a 'linear, deductive representation'] is also in question" does not mean that such an order has been totally set aside or proven irrelevant or false. But it is questioned and, by being questioned, displaced; displaced and, by being displaced, questioned. To what end? And in the service of what ends?

From the identifiable beginnings of philosophy there is the theme that thinking worthy of the name *thinking* is independent of mere causality, mere conformity to tradition ("what people say" or myth), and the motives of ulterior loss and gain (economics and politics), to name the principal aversions. These are always also within the thought and text of philosophy not as the "mere or ulterior of X" but as a part of its structure (syntax) and field of reference (words). In that sense, one might say that Derrida continues the tradition of philosophy as it might continue on against its own impurity or mixed-up-ed-ness in matters extraneous to thinking. Yet one might also say that there is nothing apart from these three factors, nothing other than a transcendent principle of right or good or truth, by which to orient ourselves philosophically; so that, if transcendence is denied or disproved, there is no orientation. Therefore philosophy sets about to assert, discover, and maintain an orientation toward these transcendental principles, however they might be formulated or reformulated from time to time. Whatever is at stake in a *philosophical* argument seems to be constrained within these elements.

In a very pertinent sense, Richard Rorty is right in claiming that all the struggles of deconstruction are local (he just seems to be misled if he implies that they are only *about* local issues). Derrida always engages a text. He does not begin with a founding statement such as "In the beginning was the Word" or its contrary "In the beginning was not the Word, but something else" or any other temporally/universally qualified assertion. Even in a text as imbued with aphorism as *Monolingualism of the Other* the aphorisms seem to oscillate:

*We only ever speak one language.*
*We never speak only one language.*

But, unlike the *aporias* of sophistic thinking, the point is not that these oppositions are situational and belong at different times or in different aspects of the same thing; rather, they are constitutive of the thing that is not a thing, the *subject who is speaking* [not a thing] and *of which they speak* [thingified]. By the time one speaks *philosophically*, there are of course already words, language, writing, and there is no pure perception, no perception that is not already mediated [here falling into a necessary solecism, since what is called "perceived" is mediated in the surrogate that does not replace anything that preceded it, "no thing" or "spirit"] in what we would call most generally words, language, writing: Words, language, writing *of the other*.

So it was with Socrates, who wanted to know what people said, which we could say is a question about what is received, transmittable, iterable, the simulacrum of an "ideal objectivity," but not finally what people said it was: the Final Truth. For if it were, why would people differ in what they said? Why would that differing already be structured not by an aboriginal "wanting to say" [*vouloir dire*] but in the resources of the medium of what they said, always and already opening and constraining a path and waiting for invention? Would one, could one, want something different? In the words recalled in a poem by an Irish poet, "Now you're supposed to be an educated man....Puzzle me the right answer to that one" (Seamus Heaney, "Casualty," *Field Work* 23).

As educated people we might hope that Derrida would puzzle us the right answer to something despite the fact that he seems always to puzzle us a further question. For those who think "philosophy" consists in questioning, this makes him philosophical; for those who think it resides in answers and the elaboration of a repeatable and reputable scheme of thought, a *program*, it is more elusive—at best a sort of wisdom literature and at worst a begging of questions. How to read Derrida *rightly* is in itself an apparently undecidable question waiting for an answer which one might hope, against odds, to decide.

# Glossary

**Aporia**: Greek term for a "puzzle" that involves what we would call a "contradiction" in terms or in Derrida's most frequent sense "undecidability" in which logic or a program of thought cannot. It is related to Derrida's use of the word path (as in :"What would be a path without aporia? *On the Name* 83) because one of its Greek meanings is "without a path" (*poros*> path, passage, ford, strait; related to terms for carrying and conducting). Derrida's *Aporias* [1993] and issues of law and politics are discussed in Beardsworth, 31-45.

**Bricolage**: From the French "bricoleur" as the name of some who uses what is at hand to fix things [an English metaphorical equivalent might be "jackdaw" after a bird that indiscriminately gathers what is available to make a nest], it was used by Levi-Strauss to characterize the assimilation of various contents in a culture and in "primitive" thinking to underlying structures. See "Structure, Sign, and Play" 255.

**Deconstruction**: In its most basic use "deconstruction" refers to a strategic demonstration that oppositional terms require each other to create the illusion of fulfillment or completeness while covering over the virtuality of the opposition in which either polar term is already implicated in and by the deployment of the other—what is excluded in the deployment of a term is always implied in its deployment without the appearance of comprehensiveness or complementarity between the two, authorizing us to say that either "state" "really exists" in the disposition described apart from our discourse or language; more generally, deconstruction refers to the demonstration that we are always in our use of language trying to achieve a "finally proper name" (*Speech and Phenomena* 160) or "total signification" which "itself always escapes" (*Speech and Phenomena* 104) articulation or determination; the term also came to be identified with modes of literary criticism (perhaps most accurately with that of Paul de Man) and eventually with all kinds of criticism including almost any kind of linguistic explication, so that its usefulness has become suspect. Derrida's *Of Grammatology* (English translation 1976) and "Structure, Sign and Play" (1970) provide a good place to begin to understand the meaning of the term as given here; it is productively revisited in John D. Caputo's *Deconstruction in a Nutshell* (1997); and it is both contextualized and given broad (perhaps too broad) application in Christopher Norris's *Deconstruction: Theory and Practice* (1982).

Glossary
"Deconstruction" implies a critique of the unity of the sign, speech-as-self-presence, the identity of language and being, etc. See also, David Wood, "Following Derrida," in Sallis, ed. 143-160.

**Differance**: An invented hybrid term, not unlike the Freudian "portmanteau," that brings together "differing" and "deferring" (signifying spatial and temporal domains) as formal requirements for the production of language: (1) all significative marks signify by their difference from other significative marks rather than by their likeness to or association with phenomena, so that their differing (spacing) is prior to their significative possibilities or functions; and (2) the "presence" of meaning is an always deferred phenomenon as each link in a significative chain, each mark, takes its meaning only in the unfolding of other oppositional marks that never fully explicate themselves but always refer beyond to what is not made present in discourse. "Differance" is not itself [sic] an entity and Derrida takes pains not to instantiate it as a "concept." (See "Differance" [1968], *Speech and Phenomena* 129-160.) A transcript of the discussion that followed the oral presentation of the 1968 essay "Differance" at the Sorbonne is reprinted in *Derrida and* Differance, ed. David Wood and Robert Bernansconi, 83-95.

**Sign [signifier, signified]**: In the *Course in General Linguistics* (65-70), Saussure analyzed the linguistic structure in which the "signifier" or "sound image" (in speech) comprises with the "signified" or "concept" the linguistic "sign"; the "signifier" is "arbitrary" in the sense that it bears no intrinsic relation to the world and is significative only by virtue a complex, but organized, set of oppositions between signifiers. This and further speculations on the nature of language (the distinction between "language" [*langue*] as a formal and impersonal system and "speaking" [*parole*] as its enactment: *Course* 77) was foundational to structural linguistics (a linguistics based on scientific principles) and, eventually, to structural anthropology (e.g., that of Claude Levi-Strauss). The analysis of the "sign" in Husserl is parallel in many respects to that in Saussure, including what Derrida critiques as a residual idealism in Saussure's account, and which he traces back to Aristotle who assumes that variation in language does not mean a variation in "mental experiences" which "are the same for all" (*De Interpretatione* 1, 16a; quoted in *Of Grammatology* 11). Characteristically, deconstruction reverses the priority or privileging of mental experience over speech and speech over writing, as it is the advent of signs that opens the possibility of any "mental experience" that we would identify with thought: Without signs ("writing" or "speech") there is (paradoxically, it would appear) no possibility of the

85

Glossary

appearance of "self-presence" because the presence in self-presence is that of a "speaking subject" to itself requiring the "supplementation" of language (also called "differance") also analogized to "auto-affection." **Speech Act Theory:** an Anglo-American development in the philosophy of language, associated with J.L. Austin and later with John R. Searle, that focuses primarily on language as a medium of communication and a means of instituting norms, based on realist assumptions about the nature of knowledge, not unlike Aristotle's assumption that "mental experiences...are the same for all" and our everyday assumption that the reality of the world and our experience of it are explicable and the accounting for the meaning of utterances is not radically problematic. From the Derridean perspective, this is perhaps more equivalent to a pragmatic theory of communication than genuine philosophical inquiry.

**Supplement [supplementation; supplementarity]:** Something can be a "supplement" to something else in the sense of being super-added to it or of filling in a lack. Writing, for instance, is conceived in Plato and others, such as Rousseau, and generally in "Western metaphysics," as something added onto primal speech (doubling its functional characteristics of signification) and something that compensates for a lack in speech (for its lack of permanence, inability to circulate). But it is also dangerous in its supplementarity to these same writers (and others such as Condillac) because it threatens to usurp and displace the "natural" relations among people and of people to themselves by, for instance, creating new possibilities of hierarchical social relation and domination from a distance; by raising new vectors of occultation and disclosure (the letter); by perverting the authenticity of face to face communication; by weakening memory through providing a prosthesis that lessens the necessity of its exercise (e.g., no one need remember names that are written down), etc. (See "...That Dangerous Supplement..." in *Of Grammatology* 141-165, and *Of Grammatology* generally.)

**Reduction [Phenomenological, Eidetic, Transcendental]:** Phenomenological reduction is a method described by Husserl of conducting "sense investigations" by radically suspending the belief that sense data presented to consciousness exist (in the sense that the datum has a corresponding material existence or existence as a substance, belongs to the world) and founding all knowledge through a presupposition-less examination of the objects of consciousness. Eidetic reduction defines idealities by the comparison and sifting of phenomena of the same class to determine what is invariable in their variability. The transcendental reduction extracts from the variation of

86

the experience of phenomena the invariability of intentionality, such that all experience takes the form of thinking is the activity of an ego thinking about something (ego cogito cogitatans) which cannot be further reduced, e.g., by analysis of the ego into parts since the ego is not experienced, only the activity of thinking (intentionality) and the object of consciousness. Husserl's method and example are important to Derrida in his attempts to conduct inquiry without metaphysical presuppositions, though Derrida does not "believe" it is possible entirely to escape, deny, or evade metaphysics. (See Velarde-Mayol, *On Husserl*, 43-53, 59-60.)

# Works Cited

Aouate, Y.C. "Les mesures d'exclusion antijuives dans l'enseignement public en Algerie (1940-1943)." *Pardes* 8 (1988).

Aristotle. *A New Aristotle Reader*. Ed. J.L. Ackrill. Princeton: Princeton UP, 1987.

Auden, W.H. *Collected Poems*. Ed. Edward Mendelson. New York: Random House, 1976.

Austin, J.L. *How to Do Things with Words*. Oxford: Oxford UP, 1963.

Beardsworth, Richard. *Derrida and the Political*. New York: Routledge, 1996.

Bennington, Geoffrey. *Interrupting Derrida*. New York: Routledge, 2000.

-------- and Jacques Derrida. *Jacques Derrida*. Trans. Geoffrey Bennington. Chicago: U of Chicago P, 1993.

Benson, Bruce Ellis. "Traces of God: The Faith of Jacques Derrida." *Books and Culture* (September/October 2000) 42-45.

Bernasconi, Robert. "Politics Beyond Humanism: Mandela and the Struggle Against Apartheid." In Madison, ed. **Working Through Derrida**: 94-119.

Bernert, Rudolf. "On Derrida's 'Introduction' to Husserl's *Origin of Geometry*." In Silverman, *Derrida and Deconstruction*: 139-153.

Biemel, Walter. "The Decisive Phases in the Development of Husserl's Philosophy." Trans. R.O. Elveton. In *The Phenomenology of Husserl: Selected Critical Readings*. Chicago: Quadrangle, 1970: 148-73.

Camus, Albert. "The Guest." *Exile and the Kingdom*. Trans. Justin O'Brien. New York: Vintage, 1991: 85-109.

Caputo, John D. *Deconstruction in a Nutshell: A Conversation with Jacques Derrida*. New York: Fordham UP, 1997.

--------. *The Prayers and Tears of Jacques Derrida: Religion without Religion*. Bloomington: Indiana UP, 1997.

Condillac, Etienne Bonnot de. *An Essay on the Origin of Human Knowledge: Being a Supplement to Mr. Locke's "Essay on the Human Understanding"* [1756]. Trans. Thomas Nugent. Gainesville: Scholars' Facsimiles and Reprints, 1971.

Culler, Jonathan. *On Deconstruction*. New York: Routledge, 1982.

Derrida, Jacques. *Acts of Literature*. Ed. Derek Attridge. New York: Routledge, 1992.

--------. *Adieu to Emmanuel Levinas*. Trans. Brault and Naas. Stanford: Stanford UP, 1999.

--------. *The Ear of the Other: Texts and Discussions with Jacques Derrida*. Ed. Christie McDonald. Trans. Peggy Kamuf. Lincoln, NE: Univ. of Nebraska P, 1982.

--------. *Edmund Husserl's "Origin of Geometry": An Introduction* [1962]. Trans. John P. Leavey, Jr. Lincoln, NE: Univ. of Nebraska P, 1989.

--------. "*Geschlect* II: Heidegger's Hand." Trans. John P. Leavey, Jr. In Sallis, ed., *Deconstruction and Philosophy*: 161-196.

--------. *The Gift of Death*. Trans. David Wills. Chicago: Univ. of Chicago P, 1995.

--------. *Glas* [1974]. Trans. John P. Leavey, Jr. and Richard Rand. Lincoln, NE: Univ. of Nebraska P, 1986.

--------. *Limited Inc*. Ed. Gerald Graff. Evanston, IL: Northwestern UP, 1988.

--------. *Margins of Philosophy* [1972]. Trans. Alan Bass. Chicago: Univ. of Chicago P, 1982.

--------. *Monolingualism of the Other; or, The Prosthesis of Origin*. Trans. Patrick Mensah. Stanford: Stanford UP, 1998.

--------. *Of Grammatology* [1967]. Trans. Gayatri Chakravorty Spivack. Baltimore: The John Hopkins UP, 1976.

--------. *Of Spirit: Heidegger and the Question*. Trans. Bennington and Bowlby. Chicago: Univ. of Chicago P, 1989.

--------. *On the Name*. Trans. Dutuit, Wood, et al. Stanford: Stanford UP, 1995.

--------. *Positions* [1972]. Trans. Alan Bass. Chicago: Univ. of Chicago P, 1981.

--------. *The Post Card* [1980]. Trans. Alan Bass. Chicago: Univ. of Chicago P, 1987.

--------. *Right of Inspection* [1985]. Trans. David Wills. New York: Monacelli, 1998.

--------. *Speech and Phenomena and Other Essays on Husserl's Theory of Signs* [1967]. Trans. David B. Allison. Evanston, IL: Northwestern UP, 1973.

--------. "Structure, Sign, and Play in the Discourse of the Human Sciences" [1966]. In Macksey and Donato, *The Structuralist Controversy*: 247-272.

--------. "White Mythology: Metaphor in the Text of Philosophy"[1971] In Derrida, *Margins of Philosophy*: 207-271.

-------- and **Gianni Vattimo**, eds. *Religion*. Stanford: Stanford UP, 1998.

"Derrida, Jacques." [**Martin C. Dillon**]. *Cambridge Dictionary of Philosophy* (2nd Edition). Ed. Robert Audi. Cambridge: Cambridge UP, 1999: 223.

**Descartes, Rene.** *Discourse on Method* [1637] and the *Meditations* [1641]. Trans. F.E. Sutcliffe. New York: Penguin, 1968.

**Eliot, T.S.** *Knowledge and Experience in the Philosophy of F.H. Bradley* [1916]. New York: Columbia UP, 1989.

--------. "Tradition and the Individual Talent" [1919]. *Selected Prose*. Ed. Frank Kermode. New York: Harcourt Brace Jovanovich, 1975: 37-44.

**Emerson, Ralph Waldo.** "Nature" [1836]. In *Ralph Waldo Emerson: Essays and Lectures*. Ed. Joel Porte. Library of America, 1983: 7-49.

**Fielding, Henry.** *Tom Jones* [1749]. Norton Critical Edition. Ed. Sheridan Baker. New York: Norton, 1973.

**Freud, Sigmund.** *Beyond the Pleasure Principle* [1920]. Trans. James Strachey. Norton, 1961.

**Heaney, Seamus.** *Field Work*. New York: Noonday, 1979.

**Heidegger, Martin.** *What is Called Thinking?* [1964]. Trans. J. Glenn Gray. New York: Harper and Row, 1968.

**Hobbes, Thomas.** *Leviathan* [1651]. Ed. J.A.C. Gaskin. New York: Oxford UP, 1996.

**Hobson, Marian.** *Jacques Derrida: Opening Lines*. New York: Routledge,

1998.

**Howells, Christina.** *Derrida: Deconstruction from Phenomenology to Ethics.* Malden, MA: Polity, 1999.

**Hume, David.** *A Treatise of Human Nature* [1739]. Ed. L.A. Selby-Bigge. Oxford: Oxford UP, 1888.

**Husserl, Edmund.** *Formal and Transcendental Logic* [1929]. Trans. Dorion Cairns. The Hague: Nijhoff, 1969.

**Johnson, Christopher.** *Derrida: The Scene of Writing.* New York: Routledge, 1999.

**Lacan, Jacques.** "Of Structure as an Inmixing of an Otherness Prerequisite to Any Subject Whatever" [1966]. In Macksey and Donato: 186-200.

**Leavey, John P., Jr.** "coda." In Derrida, *Edmund Husserl's "Origin":*183-192.

**Locke, John.** *An Essay Concerning Human Understanding* [1689]. Ed. Peter H. Nidditch. Oxford: Oxford UP, 1975.

**Macksey, Richard, and Eugenio Donato,** eds. *The Structuralist Controversy The Languages of Criticism and the Sciences of Man.* Baltimore: The Johns Hopkins UP, 1972.

**Madison, Gary B.,** ed. *Working through Derrida.* Evanston, IL: Northwestern UP, 1993.

**Milton, John.** *Selected Prose.* Ed. C.A. Patrides. Baltimore: Penguin Books, 1974.

**Mouffe, Chantal,** ed. *Deconstruction and Pragmatism.* New York: Routledge, 1996.

--------. "Deconstruction, Pragmatism, and Democracy." In Mouffe, ed. *Deconstruction and Pragmatism*: 1-12.

**Norris, Christopher.** *Deconstruction: Theory and Practice.* New York: Methuen, 1982.

--------. *Derrida.* Cambridge: Harvard UP, 1987.

**Rorty, Richard.** "Remarks on Deconstruction and Pragmatism." In Mouffe, ed. *Deconstruction and Pragmatism*: 13-18.

**Sallis, John,** ed. *Deconstruction and Philosophy: The Texts of Jacques Derrida.* Chicago: Univ. of Chicago P, 1987.

**Saussure, Ferdinand de.** *Course in General Linguistics* [1915]. Trans. Wade Baskin. New York: McGraw-Hill, 1966.

**Searle, John R.** "Reiterating the Differences: A Reply to Derrida." *Glyph* I (1977): 198-208.

--------. "The World Turned Upside Down" [*New York Review of Books,* October 27, 1983]. In Madison, *Working Through Derrida*: 170-183.

**Silverman, Hugh J.,** ed. *Derrida and Deconstruction.* New York: Routledge, 1989.

**Strathern, Paul.** *Derrida in 90 Minutes.* Chicago: Dee, 2000.

**Velarde-Mayol, Victor.** *On Husserl.* Belmont, CA: Wadsworth, 2000.

**Wood, David.** "Following Derrida." In Sallis, ed. *Deconstruction and Philosophy*: 143-60.

-------- **and Robert Bernasconi,** eds. *Derrida and* Differance. Evanston, IL: Northwestern UP, 1988.